WHAT IS OVERLAY CROCHET?

Overlay crochet is a technique that takes crochet into a new dimension—REALLY! Layers of stitches add depth and volume to make the usual into the unique. With projects inspired by mandalas, bright color can be added in small touches or be used throughout.

IT IS ALL UP TO YOU!

LEISURE ARTS, INC. • Maumelle, Arkansas

KRISTI SIMPSON

Inspired by her love of yarn, Kristi Simpson creates crochet and knit patterns with a fresh and modern touch. The mother of five became hooked on crochet after teaching herself so she could help her daughter make a scarf from a "learn to crochet" kit that was a gift.

"I loved it from the beginning," she says. "I was amazed that I could take a string of yarn and create something so useful and pretty! Needless to say, I never stopped!"

Look for other Leisure Arts books featuring Kristi's designs at www.leisurearts.com/meet-the-designers/kristi-simpson.html.

Visit kristisimpson.net or find her on Ravelry, Facebook, and Pinterest.

BASKET

Finished Size:
9½" long x 7" wide x 3¾" deep
(24 cm x 18 cm x 9.5 cm)

SHOPPING LIST

Yarn (Medium Weight)

[3.5 ounces, 153 yards
(100 grams, 140 meters) per skein]:
☐ Coral - 1 skein
☐ Blue - 1 skein
☐ Cream - 1 skein

Crochet Hook
☐ Size G (4 mm)
  or size needed for gauge

GAUGE INFORMATION

In Bottom pattern,
  17 sc and 19 rows = 4" (10 cm)
Gauge Swatch: 6½" wide x 4" high
  (16.5 cm x 10 cm)
Work same as Bottom through Row 19,
do **not** finish off: 28 sc.

STITCH GUIDE

PUFF STITCH *(abbreviated Puff St)* (uses one sc)
★ YO, insert hook in sc indicated, YO and pull up loop; repeat from
★ 2 times **more** (7 loops on hook), YO and draw through all 7 loops on
hook, ch 1 to close.

FRONT POST DOUBLE CROCHET *(abbreviated FPdc)*
Working in **front** of previous rnds, YO, insert hook from **front** to **back**
around post of st indicated *(Fig. 5, page 61)*, YO and pull up a loop
(3 loops on hook), (YO and draw through 2 loops on hook) twice. Skip sc
behind FPdc.

DOUBLE CROCHET 2 TOGETHER *(abbreviated dc2tog)* (uses next 2 sts)
★ YO, insert hook in **next** st, YO and pull up a loop, YO and draw through
2 loops on hook; repeat from ★ once **more**, YO and draw through all
3 loops on hook (**counts as one dc**).

DOUBLE CROCHET 3 TOGETHER *(abbreviated dc3tog)* (uses next 3 sts)
★ YO, insert hook in **next** st, YO and pull up a loop, YO and draw through
2 loops on hook; repeat from ★ 2 times **more**, YO and draw through all
4 loops on hook (**counts as one dc**).

BOTTOM

With Coral, ch 29.

Row 1: Sc in second ch from hook and in
each across: 28 sc.

Row 2 (Right side)**:** Ch 1, turn; sc in each
sc across.

Note: Loop a short piece of yarn around
any stitch to mark Row 2 as **right** side.

Rows 3-42: Ch 1, turn; sc in each sc
across.

Do **not** finish off.

TRIM

Ch 1, do **not** turn; † skip first row, sc in end of next row and in each row across to last row, skip last row †; working in free loops of beginning ch *(Fig. 4b, page 61)*, 3 sc in ch at base of first sc on Row 1, sc in next 26 chs, 3 sc in last ch; repeat from † to † once; 3 sc in first sc on Row 42, sc in next 26 sc, 3 sc in last sc; join with slip st to first sc, finish off: 144 sc.

SIDES

Rnd 1: With **right** side facing and working in Back Loops Only *(Fig. 3, page 60)*, join Cream with slip st in center sc of of last 3-sc group on Trim, ch 2 **(counts as first hdc, now and throughout)**, sc in next 42 sc, hdc in next sc, sc in next 28 sc, hdc in next sc, sc in next 42 sc, hdc in next sc, sc in next 28 sc; join with slip st to first hdc: 140 sc and 4 corner hdc.

Rnd 2: Ch 2, working in Back Loops Only, sc in each sc across to next corner hdc, (hdc in corner hdc, sc in each sc across to next corner hdc) around; join with slip st to **both** loops of first hdc changing to Blue *(Fig. 6a, page 61)*, cut Cream.

Rnd 3: Ch 3 **(counts as first hdc plus ch 1)**, skip next sc, work Puff St in next sc, ★ † (ch 1, skip next sc, work Puff St in next sc) across to next corner hdc †, hdc in corner hdc; repeat from ★ 2 times **more**, then repeat from † to † once; join with slip st to first hdc changing to Cream, cut Blue: 74 sts and 70 ch-1 sps.

Rnd 4: Ch 2, working **around** next ch *(Fig. 8, page 62)*, dc in skipped sc on Rnd 2, sc in top of next Puff St, (working **around** next ch, dc in skipped sc on Rnd 2, sc in top of next Puff St) across

to next corner hdc, ★ hdc in corner hdc, (working **around** next ch, dc in skipped sc **below** ch, sc in top of next Puff St) across to next corner hdc; repeat from ★ around; join with slip st to Back Loop Only of first hdc: 144 sts.

Rnd 5: Ch 2, working in Back Loops Only, sc in each st across to next corner hdc, (hdc in corner hdc, sc in each sc across to next corner hdc) around; join with slip st to **both** loops of first hdc.

Rnd 6: Ch 2, (work FPdc around next dc on Rnd 4, sc in next sc) across to next corner hdc, ★ hdc in corner hdc, (work FPdc around next dc on Rnd 4, sc in next sc) across to next corner hdc; repeat from ★ around; join with slip st to first hdc.

Rnd 7: Ch 2, sc in each st across to next corner hdc, (hdc in corner hdc, sc in each st across to next corner hdc) around; join with slip st to first hdc.

Rnd 8: Ch 2, (sc in next sc, work FPdc around next sc on Rnd 6) across to next corner hdc, ★ hdc in corner hdc, (sc in next sc, work FPdc around next sc on Rnd 6) across to next corner hdc; repeat from ★ around; join with slip st to first hdc.

Rnd 9: Repeat Rnd 7.

Rnd 10: Ch 2, (work FPdc around next sc on Rnd 8, sc in next sc) across to next corner hdc, ★ hdc in corner hdc, (work FPdc around next sc on Rnd 8, sc in next sc) across to next corner hdc; repeat from ★ around; join with slip st to first hdc.

Rnd 11: Ch 2, † [skip next 2 sts, (sc, ch 2, sc) in next st] 13 times, ch 1, skip next 3 sts, hdc in next corner hdc, [skip next 2 sts, (sc, ch 2, sc) in next st] 9 times, skip next sc †, hdc in next corner hdc; repeat from † to † once; join with slip st to first hdc: 92 sts and 46 sps.

Rnd 12: Ch 2, skip next sc, † sc in next ch-2 sp, [skip next 2 sc, 7 dc in next ch-2 sp, skip next 2 sc, sc in next ch-2 sp] 6 times, skip next sc and next ch-1 sp, hdc in next corner hdc, skip next sc, sc in next ch-2 sp, [skip next 2 sc, 7 dc in next ch-2 sp, skip next 2 sc, sc in next ch-2 sp] 4 times, skip next sc †, hdc in next corner hdc, repeat from † to † once; join with slip st to first hdc: 168 sts.

Rnd 13: Ch 2, † dc2tog, hdc in next dc, sc in next 3 dc, hdc in next dc, (dc3tog, hdc in next dc, sc in next 3 dc, hdc in next dc) 5 times, (dc2tog, hdc in next st) twice, sc in next 3 dc, hdc in next dc, (dc3tog, hdc in next dc, sc in next 3 dc, hdc in next dc) 3 times, dc2tog †, hdc in next hdc; repeat from † to † once; join with slip st to first hdc: 128 sts.

Rnd 14: Ch 2, † sc in next 37 sts, hdc in next corner hdc, sc in next 25 sts †, hdc in next corner hdc; repeat from † to † once; join with slip st to first hdc changing to Blue, do **not** cut Cream.

Rnd 15: Ch 2, hdc in next st and in each st around; join with slip st to first hdc changing to Cream, cut Blue.

Rnd 16: Ch 2, working in horizontal bar of hdc *(Fig. 9, page 62)*, hdc in next hdc and each hdc around; join with slip st to first hdc, finish off.

Rnd 17: With **right** side facing, join Coral with slip st in first hdc; slip st in each st around; join with slip st to first slip st, finish off.

BLANKET

●●○○ EASY

Finished Size: 26" x 42"
(66 cm x 106.5 cm)

SHOPPING LIST

Yarn (Medium Weight)
[1.75 ounces, 84 yards
(50 grams, 77 meters) per skein]:
- ☐ White - 6 skeins
- ☐ Aqua - 3 skeins
- ☐ Coral - 3 skeins
- ☐ Yellow - 3 skeins

Crochet Hook
- ☐ Size J (6 mm)
  or size needed for gauge

GAUGE INFORMATION
Each Square = 8" (20.5 cm) square
Gauge Swatch: 4" (10 cm) square
Work same as Square C on page 13
through Rnd 3: 20 tr, 4 slip sts, and
8 ch-3 sps.

STITCH GUIDE
TREBLE CROCHET *(abbreviated tr)*
YO twice, insert hook in st indicated, YO and pull up a loop (4 loops on hook),
(YO and draw through 2 loops on hook) 3 times.
BEGINNING CLUSTER (uses one st)
Ch 2, ★ YO, insert hook in st indicated, YO and pull up a loop, YO and draw
through 2 loops on hook; repeat from ★ once **more**, YO and draw through all
3 loops on hook.
CLUSTER (uses one st)
★ YO, insert hook in st indicated, YO and pull up a loop, YO and draw through
2 loops on hook; repeat from ★ 2 times **more**, YO and draw through all 4 loops
on hook.
DOUBLE CROCHET 3 TOGETHER *(abbreviated dc3tog)* (uses 2 sts)
YO, insert hook in **same** st as last st made, YO and pull up a loop, YO and draw
through 2 loops on hook, ★ YO, insert hook in **next** st, YO and pull up a loop,
YO and draw through 2 loops on hook; repeat from ★ once **more**, YO and draw
through all 4 loops on hook (**counts as one dc**).
PUFF STITCH *(abbreviated Puff St)* (uses one ch-1 sp)
★ YO, insert hook in sp indicated, YO and pull up a loop; repeat from ★ 3 times
more (9 loops on hook), YO and draw through all 9 loops on hook, ch 1 to close.
SPLIT FRONT POST TREBLE CROCHET *(abbreviated split FPtr)* (uses 2 sc)
First Leg: YO twice, insert hook from **front** to **back** around post of sc indicated
(Fig. 5, page 61), YO and pull up a loop (4 loops on hook), (YO and draw through
2 loops on hook) twice (2 loops on hook).
Second Leg: YO twice, skip next 3 sts from First Leg, insert hook from **front** to **back**
around post of next sc, YO and pull up a loop, (YO and draw through 2 loops on
hook) twice, YO and draw through all 3 loops on hook (**counts as one st**).
BACK POST SINGLE CROCHET *(abbreviated BPsc)*
Insert hook from **back** to **front** around post of st indicated *(Fig. 5, page 61)*, YO and
pull up a loop (2 loops on hook), YO and draw through both loops on hook.
FRONT POST SINGLE CROCHET *(abbreviated FPsc)*
Insert hook from **front** to **back** around post of st indicated *(Fig. 5, page 61)*, YO and
pull up a loop (2 loops on hook), YO and draw through both loops on hook.
FRONT POST DOUBLE CROCHET *(abbreviated FPdc)*
YO, insert hook from **front** to **back** around post of st indicated *(Fig. 5, page 61)*,
YO and pull up a loop (3 loops on hook), (YO and draw through 2 loops on
hook) twice.
FRONT POST TREBLE CROCHET *(abbreviated FPtr)*
YO twice, insert hook from **front** to **back** around st indicated *(Fig. 5, page 61)*,
YO and pull up a loop (4 loops on hook), (YO and draw through 2 loops on hook)
3 times.

Work with **right** side facing throughout.

SQUARE A (Make 6)

Rnd 1 (Right side)**:** With White, ch 2, 8 sc in second ch from hook; join with slip st to first sc, finish off.

Note: Loop a short piece of yarn around any stitch to mark Rnd 1 as **right** side.

Rnd 2: Join Aqua with slip st in any sc; work Beginning Cluster in same st, ch 1, (work Cluster in next sc, ch 1) around; join with slip st to top of Beginning Cluster, finish off: 8 Clusters and 8 ch-1 sps.

Rnd 3: Join Coral with dc in any ch-1 sp; *(see Joining With Dc, page 60)*; 2 dc in same sp, ch 1, (3 dc in next ch-1 sp, ch 1) around; join with slip st to first dc, finish off: 24 dc and 8 ch-1 sps.

Rnd 4: Join White with slip st in center dc of any 3-dc group; working in **front** of next ch-1 sp *(Fig. 8, page 62)*, (dc, ch 1, dc) in top of Cluster on Rnd 2, place marker around ch-1 sp just made for st placement, ★ skip next dc on Rnd 3,

slip st in next dc, working in **front** of next ch-1 sp, (dc, ch 1, dc) in top of Cluster on Rnd 2; repeat from ★ around; join with slip st to first slip st, finish off: 16 dc and 8 chs.

Rnd 5: Holding Rnd 3 **behind** Rnd 4 and working through **both** layers, join Yellow with slip st in marked ch-1 sp; remove marker; ch 2 **(does not count as a st)**, work Puff St in same sp, ch 4, ★ working through **both** layers, work Puff St in next ch-1 sp, ch 4; repeat from ★ around; join with slip st to top of first Puff St, finish off: 8 Puff Sts and 8 ch-4 sps.

Rnd 6: Working **around** any ch-4 on Rnd 5, join Coral with dc in slip st on Rnd 4 **below**; 4 dc in same st, slip st in top of next Puff St, ★ working **around** next ch-4, 5 dc in slip st on Rnd 4 **below**, slip st in top of next Puff St; repeat from ★ around; join with slip st to first dc, finish off: 40 dc and 8 slip sts.

Rnd 7: Join Aqua with dc **around** any slip st and in top of Puff St **below**; 6 dc in same st, ch 3, slip st in Back Loop Only of next slip st *(Fig. 3, page 60)*; ch 3, ★ working **around** next slip st, 7 dc in

top of Puff St **below**, ch 3, slip st in Back Loop Only of next slip st, ch 3; repeat from ★ around; join with slip st to first dc, finish off: 28 dc, 8 ch-3 sps, and 4 slip sts.

Rnd 8: Join White with dc **around** any slip st on Rnd 6 in top of Puff St **below**; (2 dc, ch 2, 3 dc) in same st, ch 3, working **behind** next 7-dc group, slip st around loops on back of next Puff St **below**, ch 3, ★ working **around** next slip st on Rnd 6 and in top of Puff St **below**, (3 dc, ch 2, 3 dc) in same st, ch 3, working **behind** next 7-dc group, slip st around loops on back of next Puff St **below**, ch 3; repeat from ★ 2 times **more**; join with slip st to first dc, finish off: 24 dc, 4 slip sts, and 12 sps.

Rnd 9: Join Coral with dc in any corner ch-2 sp; (2 dc, ch 1, 3 dc) in same sp, ch 4, working **behind** next 7-dc group on Rnd 7, slip st in next slip st, ch 4, ★ (3 dc, ch 1, 3 dc) in next corner ch-2 sp, ch 4, working **behind** next 7-dc group on Rnd 7, slip st in next slip st, ch 4; repeat from ★ around; join with slip st to first dc, finish off.

Rnd 10: Join White with sc in any corner ch-1 sp *(see Joining With Sc, page 60)*; sc in same sp and in next 3 dc, ★ † working **around** chs of last 2 rnds, 5 dc in next sp, slip st in center dc of next 7-dc group on Rnd 7, working **around** chs of last 2 rnds, 5 dc in next sp, sc in next 3 dc †, 3 sc in next corner ch-1 sp, sc in next 3 dc; repeat from ★ 2 times **more**, then repeat from † to † once, sc in same sp as first sc; join with slip st to first sc, do **not** finish off: 80 sts.

Rnd 11: Ch 3 **(counts as first dc, now and throughout)**, 2 dc in same st as joining, (dc in next 19 sts, 3 dc in next sc) 3 times, dc in last 19 sts; join with slip st to first dc: 88 dc.

Rnd 12: Ch 1, sc in same st as joining and in next dc, 3 sc in next dc, (sc in next 21 dc, 3 sc in next dc) 3 times, sc in last 19 dc; join with slip st to first sc, finish off: 96 sc.

SQUARE B (Make 6)

Rnd 1 (Right side): With Coral, ch 4, 15 dc in fourth ch from hook (**3 skipped chs count as first dc**); join with slip st to first dc, finish off: 16 dc.

Note: Mark Rnd 1 as **right** side.

Rnd 2: Join Aqua with slip st in any dc; slip st in next dc and in each dc around; join with slip st to joining slip st, finish off.

Rnd 3: Working in Back Loops Only, join White with dc in any dc on Rnd 1; 2 dc in next dc, (dc in next dc, 2 dc in next dc) around; join with slip st to **both** loops of first dc, finish off: 24 dc.

Rnd 4: Join Yellow with sc in same st as joining; place marker in sc just made for st placement, sc in next dc, working in free loops of dc on Rnd 1 (*Fig. 4a, page 61*), YO, insert hook in dc **below** first sc, YO and pull up a loop, YO and draw through 2 loops on hook, (YO, insert hook in **next** dc, YO and pull up a loop, YO and draw through 2 loops on hook) twice, YO and draw through all 4 loops on hook (**counts as one dc**), sc in next 3 dc, (dc3tog, sc in next 3 dc) around to last dc, dc3tog working last leg in same dc as first dc3tog, sc in last dc; join with slip st to first sc changing to White (*Fig. 6a, page 61*), cut Yellow: 32 sts.

Rnd 5: Ch 3, dc in next sc, 2 dc in next dc, (dc in next 3 sc, 2 dc in next dc) around to last sc, dc in last sc; join with slip st to first dc changing to Coral, cut White: 40 dc.

Rnd 6: Ch 1, sc in same st and in next 2 dc, work First Leg of split FPtr around marked sc, do **not** remove marker, ★ work Second Leg, skip next dc from last sc made, sc in next 4 dc, working **below** Second Leg, work First Leg of split FPtr around same st; repeat from ★ around to last 2 dc, work Second Leg around marked sc **above** First Leg of first split FPtr, remove marker, skip next dc from last sc made, sc in last dc; join with slip st to first sc, finish off.

Rnd 7: Skip first sc and join Aqua with dc in next sc; 5 dc in same st, skip next sc, work FPsc around next split FPtr, ★ skip next 2 sc, 6 dc in next sc, skip next sc, work FPsc around next split FPtr; repeat from ★ around; join with slip st to first dc, finish off: 48 dc and 8 FPsc.

Rnd 8: Skip first 3 dc of any 6-dc group and join Yellow with sc in sp **before** next dc (*Fig. 7, page 62*); ch 3, dc in next FPsc, ch 3, ★ skip next 3 dc, sc in sp **before** next dc, ch 3, dc in next FPsc, ch 3; repeat from ★ around; join with slip st to first sc, do **not** finish off: 16 sts and 16 ch-3 sps.

Rnd 9: Ch 1, sc in same st as joining, 3 sc in next ch-3 sp, 2 sc in next dc, 3 sc in next ch-3 sp, ★ sc in next sc, 3 sc in next ch-3 sp, 2 sc in next dc, 3 sc in next ch-3 sp; repeat from ★ around; join with slip st to first sc changing to White, cut Yellow: 72 sc.

Rnd 10: Ch 1, sc in same st as joining and in next 8 sc, ★ † dc in next 2 sc, tr in next 2 sc, (2 tr, ch 1, 2 tr) in next sc, tr in next 2 sc, dc in next 2 sc †, sc in next 9 sc; repeat from ★ 2 times **more**, then repeat from † to † once; join with slip st to first sc, do **not** finish off: 84 sts and 4 corner ch-1 sps.

Rnd 11: Ch 1, sc in same st as joining and in each st around working 3 sc in each corner ch-1 sp; join with slip st to first sc, finish off: 96 sc.

SQUARE C (Make 3)

Rnd 1 (Right side): With Yellow, ch 4, 2 dc in fourth ch from hook (**3 skipped chs count as first dc**), ch 3, (3 dc in same ch, ch 3) 3 times; join with slip st to first dc, finish off: 12 dc and 4 corner ch-3 sps.

Note: Mark Rnd 1 as **right** side.

Rnd 2: Join Coral with dc in any corner ch-3 sp; (2 dc, ch 3, 3 dc) in same sp, ch 2, ★ (3 dc, ch 3, 3 dc) in next corner ch-3 sp, ch 2; repeat from ★ 2 times **more**; join with slip st to first dc, finish off: 24 dc and 8 sps.

Rnd 3: Join Aqua with slip st in any corner ch-3 sp; ch 3, working **around** next ch-2, 5 tr in center dc of 3-dc group **below**, ch 3, ★ slip st in next corner ch-3 sp, ch 3, working **around** next ch-2, 5 tr in center dc of 3-dc group **below**, ch 3; repeat from ★ 2 times **more**; join with slip st to joining slip st, finish off: 20 tr, 4 slip sts, and 8 ch-3 sps.

Rnd 4: Join White with dc in any corner ch-3 sp on Rnd 2 and working **around** slip st; (2 dc, ch 3, 3 dc) in same sp, ch 1, work BPsc around each of next 5 tr, ch 1, ★ (3 dc, ch 3, 3 dc) in next corner ch-3 sp on Rnd 2 **around** slip st, ch 1, work BPsc around each of next 5 tr, ch 1; repeat from ★ 2 times **more**; join with slip st to first dc, finish off: 24 dc, 20 BPsc, and 12 sps.

Rnd 5: Join Coral with sc in any corner ch-3 sp; 2 sc in same sp, ★ † sc in next 3 dc, skip next ch-1 sp, sc in next 2 BPsc, working **below** next BPsc, work (FPdc, ch 2, FPdc) around same st, skip BPsc from last sc made, sc in next 2 BPsc, skip next ch-1 sp, sc in next 3 dc †, 3 sc in next corner ch-3 sp; repeat from ★ 2 times **more**, then repeat from † to † once; join with slip st to first sc, finish off: 52 sc, 8 FPdc, and 4 ch-2 sps.

Rnd 6: Join Yellow with slip st in Back Loop Only of first FPdc; ★ † ch 3, slip st in Back Loop Only of next FPdc, ch 6, working **behind** previous rnds, slip st in corner ch-3 sp on Rnd 2 **between** 3-dc groups, working **behind** previous rnds, ch 6 †, slip st in Back Loop Only of next FPdc; repeat from ★ 2 times **more**, then repeat from † to † once; join with slip st to first slip st, do **not** finish off: 12 slip sts and 12 sps.

Rnd 7: Slip st around next ch-3 sp on Rnd 6 **and** in ch-2 sp on Rnd 5; ch 1, 4 hdc in same sp, 7 hdc in each of next 2 ch-6 sps, ★ working around next ch-3 sp on Rnd 6 **and** in ch-2 sp on Rnd 5, 4 hdc in next sp, 7 hdc in each of next 2 ch-6 sps; repeat from ★ 2 times **more**; join with slip st to first hdc, finish off: 72 hdc.

Rnd 8: Working **around** previous rnds, join Aqua with slip st in corner slip st on Rnd 6; work (Beginning Cluster, ch 1, Cluster, ch 2, Cluster, ch 1, Cluster) in same st, ★ † skip next 3 hdc, work BPdc around next 2 hdc, work BPsc around next 8 hdc, work BPdc around next 2 hdc, skip next 3 hdc †, working **around** previous rnds, work (Cluster, ch 1, Cluster, ch 2, Cluster, ch 1, Cluster) in corner slip st on Rnd 6; repeat from ★ 2 times **more**, then repeat from † to † once; join with slip st to top of Beginning Cluster, finish off: 32 BPsc, 16 BPdc, and 16 Clusters.

Rnd 9: Join White with sc in any corner ch-2 sp; 2 sc in same sp, ★ † sc in top of next Cluster, sc in next ch-1 sp and in top of next Cluster, 2 sc in next FPdc, sc in next 12 sts, sc in next ch-1 sp and in top of next Cluster †, 3 sc in next corner ch-2 sp; repeat from ★ 2 times **more**, then repeat from † to † once; join with slip st to first sc, do **not** finish off: 88 sc.

Rnd 10: Ch 1, sc in same st as joining, 3 sc in next sc, (sc in next 21 sc, 3 sc in next sc) 3 times, sc in last 20 sc; join with slip st to first sc, finish off: 96 sc.

DIAGRAM

A	B	C
B	A	B
A	C	A
B	A	B
C	B	A

FINISHING

Following Diagram on page 14 for placement, with **wrong** sides together, and working through **inside** loops only, slip st Squares together using White, beginning in center sc of first corner 3-sc group and in ending center sc of next corner 3-sc group, forming 3 vertical strips of 5 Squares **each**, then slip st strips together in same manner.

BORDER

Rnd 1: Join Aqua with dc in center sc of corner 3-sc group on short edge of Blanket; ch 2, dc in same st, skip next sc, (dc, ch 1, dc) in next sc, † [skip next 2 sc, (dc, ch 1, dc) in next sc] across to next seam, skip seam and next sc, (dc, ch 1, dc) in next sc †; repeat from † to † once **more**, [skip next 2 sc, (dc, ch 1, dc) in next sc] across to within 3 sc of next corner sc, [skip next sc, (dc, ch 2, dc) in next sc] 3 times, repeat from † to † 4 times, [skip next 2 sc, (dc, ch 1, dc) in next sc] across to within 3 sc of next corner sc, [skip next sc, (dc, ch 2, dc) in next sc] 3 times, repeat from † to † twice, [skip next 2 sc, (dc, ch 1, dc) in next sc] across to within 3 sc of next corner sc, [skip next sc, (dc, ch 2, dc) in next sc] 3 times, repeat from † to † 4 times, [skip next 2 sc, (dc, ch 1, dc) in next sc] 6 times, skip last sc; join with slip to first dc, finish off.

Rnd 2: Join White with sc in any corner ch-2 sp; (ch 2, 2 sc, ch 2, sc) in same sp, (sc, ch 2, sc) in each ch-1 sp across to next corner ch-2 sp, ★ (sc, ch 2, 2 sc, ch 2, sc) in corner ch-2 sp, (sc, ch 2, sc) in each ch-1 sp across to next corner ch-2 sp; repeat from ★ 2 times **more**, (sc, ch 2, sc) in each ch-1 sp across; join with slip st to first sc, finish off.

CROSSBODY BAG

●●○○ EASY

Finished Size: 10" (25.5 cm) diameter

SHOPPING LIST

Yarn (Medium Weight)
[1.75 ounces, 80 yards
(50 grams, 73 meters) per skein]:
- ☐ Violet - 2 skeins
- ☐ Coral - 1 skein
- ☐ Yellow - 1 skein
- ☐ Cream - 1 skein

Crochet Hook
- ☐ Size H (5 mm)
  or size needed for gauge

Additional Supplies
- ☐ Yarn needle
- ☐ Safety pin
- ☐ Fabric glue
- ☐ Hook and loop fastener strip

GAUGE INFORMATION
Gauge Swatch: 5" (12.75 cm) diameter
Work same as Front on page 18 through
Rnd 9: 64 sts.

STITCH GUIDE
TREBLE CROCHET *(abbreviated tr)*
YO twice, insert hook in st indicated, YO and pull up a loop (4 loops on hook), (YO and draw through 2 loops on hook) 3 times.

BACK POST SINGLE CROCHET *(abbreviated BPsc)*
Insert hook from **back** to **front** around post of st indicated *(Fig. 5, page 61)*, YO and pull up a loop (2 loops on hook), YO and draw through both loops on hook.

FRONT POST SINGLE CROCHET *(abbreviated FPsc)*
Insert hook from **front** to **back** around post of st indicated *(Fig. 5, page 61)*, YO and pull up a loop (2 loops on hook), YO and draw through both loops on hook.

FRONT POST DOUBLE CROCHET *(abbreviated FPdc)*
YO, insert hook from **front** to **back** around post of st indicated *(Fig. 5, page 61)*, YO and pull up a loop (3 loops on hook), (YO and draw through 2 loops on hook) twice.

FRONT POST TREBLE CROCHET *(abbreviated FPtr)*
YO twice, insert hook from **front** to **back** around post of st indicated *(Fig. 5, page 61)*, YO and pull up a loop (4 loops on hook), (YO and draw through 2 loops on hook) 3 times.

SPLIT FRONT POST TREBLE CROCHET *(abbreviated split FPtr)*
First Leg: Working in **front** of previous rnds, YO twice, insert hook from **front** to **back** around post of st indicated *(Fig. 5, page 61)*, YO and pull up a loop (4 loops on hook), (YO and draw through 2 loops on hook) twice (2 loops on hook).
Second Leg: YO twice, insert hook from **front** to **back** around post of next FPtr, YO and pull up a loop, (YO and draw through 2 loops on hook) twice, YO and draw through all 3 loops on hook (**counts as one st**).

FRONT

Rnd 1 (Right side)**:** With Violet, ch 4, 7 dc in fourth ch from hook **(3 skipped chs count as first dc, now and throughout)**; join with slip st to first dc changing to Coral **(Fig. 6a, page 61)**, cut Violet: 8 dc.

Note: Loop a short piece of yarn around any stitch to mark Rnd 1 as **right** side.

Rnd 2: Working in Back Loops Only **(Fig. 3, page 60)**, ch 1, sc in same st, work FPdc around same st, place marker around st just made for st placement, ★ sc in Back Loop Only of next dc, work FPdc around same st; repeat from ★ around; join with slip st to first sc changing to Yellow, cut Coral: 16 sts.

Rnd 3: Ch 1, working in Back Loops Only, sc in same st as joining, 2 sc in next FPdc, (sc in next sc, 2 sc in next FPdc) around; join with slip st to first sc: 24 sc.

Rnd 4: Ch 1, working in Back Loops Only, sc in same st as joining and in next sc, 2 sc in next sc, (sc in next 2 sc, 2 sc in next sc) around; join with slip st to first sc: 32 sc.

Rnd 5: Ch 1, working in Back Loops Only, sc in same st as joining and in next 2 sc, 2 sc in next sc, (sc in next 3 sc, 2 sc in next sc) around; join with slip st to first sc, place loop from hook onto safety pin to keep piece from unraveling while working next rnd: 40 sc.

Rnd 6: With **right** side facing, join Coral with slip st around post of marked FPdc on Rnd 2; ch 7 **(counts as first FPtr plus ch 3)**, (work FPtr around next FPdc, ch 3) around; join with slip st to first FPtr, finish off: 8 FPtr and 8 ch-3 sps.

Rnd 7: Slip loop from safety pin onto hook, ch 1, working **around** first ch-3 on Rnd 6 *(Fig. 8, page 62)* and in Back Loops Only of sc on Rnd 5, sc in same st as joining on Rnd 5 and in next sc, 2 sc in next sc, sc in next 2 sc, skip next FPtr, ★ sc in next 2 sc, 2 sc in next sc, sc in next 2 sc, skip next FPtr; repeat from ★ around to last 2 sc, sc in last 2 sc; join with slip st to first sc changing to Coral, cut Yellow: 48 sc.

Rnd 8: Ch 1, working in Back Loops Only, sc in same st as joining and in next 2 sc, work First Leg of split FPtr around first FPtr, ★ work Second Leg of split FPtr, sc in next 6 sc, working **below** Second Leg of last split FPtr made, work First Leg of split FPtr; repeat from ★ around, working Second Leg of last split FPtr **above** First Leg of first split FPtr, sc in last 3 sc; join with slip st to first sc changing to Violet, cut Coral: 48 sc and 8 split FPtr.

Rnd 9: Ch 1, working in Back Loops Only, sc in same st as joining and in next 2 sc, work FPsc around next split FPtr, sc in next 3 sc, work FPtr around next FPtr on Rnd 6 (**above** legs of split FPtr), ★ sc in next 3 sc, work FPsc around next split FPtr, sc in next 3 sc, work FPtr around next FPtr on Rnd 6 (**above** legs of split FPtr); repeat from ★ around; join with slip st to first sc, finish off: 64 sts.

Rnd 10: With **right** side facing and working in Back Loops Only, join Cream with sc in any FPsc *(see Joining With Sc, page 60)*; sc in same st and in next 6 sts, (2 sc in next FPsc, sc in next 7 sts) around; join with slip st to first sc, do **not** finish off: 72 sc.

Rnd 11: Ch 1, working in Back Loops Only, sc in same st as joining, 2 sc in next sc, (sc in next 8 sc, 2 sc in next sc) around to last 7 sc, sc in last 7 sc; join with slip st to first sc changing to Yellow, cut Cream: 80 sc.

Rnd 12: Ch 1, working in Back Loops Only, sc in same st as joining and in each sc around; join with slip st to first sc changing to Violet, cut Yellow.

Rnd 13: Working in Back Loops Only, slip st in same st as joining; sc in next sc, dc in next 2 sc, 2 tr in next sc, dc in next 2 sc, sc in next sc, ★ slip st in next 2 sc, sc in next sc, dc in next 2 sc, 2 tr in next sc, tr in next sc, dc in next 2 sc, sc in next sc; repeat from ★ around to last sc, slip st in last sc; join with slip st to first slip st changing to Coral, cut Violet: 88 sts.

Rnd 14: Ch 1, work BPsc around same st as joining and each st around; join with slip to Back Loop Only of first BPsc changing to Cream, cut Coral.

Rnd 15: Ch 1, working in Back Loops Only, sc in same st as joining, skip next BPsc, sc in next BPsc and in each BPsc around; join with slip st to **both** loops of first sc, finish off: 87 sc.

Rnd 16: With **right** side facing and working in both loops, join Yellow with dc in same st as joining *(see Joining With Dc, page 60)*; 2 dc in same st, ch 1, skip next 2 sc, ★ 3 dc in next sc, ch 1, skip next 2 sc; repeat from ★ around; join with slip st to first dc, finish off: 87 dc and 29 ch-1 sps.

Rnd 17: With **right** side facing, join Violet with slip st in center dc of any 3-dc group, working in **front** of next ch-1, dc in second skipped sc **below** ch-1, ch 1, working in **front** of dc just made, dc in first skipped sc, ★ slip st in center dc of next 3-dc group, working in **front** of next ch-1, dc in second skipped sc **below** ch-1, ch 1, working in **front** of dc just made, dc in first skipped sc; repeat from ★ around; join with slip st to first slip st changing to Coral, cut Violet.

Rnd 18: Ch 1, sc in same st as joining and in next dc, working through **both** sps, sc in next ch-1 sp **and** in ch-1 sp on Rnd 16, sc in next dc, ★ sc in next slip st and in next dc, working through **both** sps, sc in next ch-1 sp **and** in ch-1 sp on Rnd 16, sc in next dc; repeat from ★ around; join with slip st to first sc, finish off: 116 sc.

BACK

Rnd 1 (Right side)**:** With Violet, ch 4, 7 dc in third ch from hook; join with slip st to first dc.

Note: Mark Rnd 1 as **right** side.

Work in Back Loops Only through Rnd 13.

Rnd 2: Ch 1, 2 sc in same st as joining and in each dc around, do **not** join, place marker to indicate beginning of rnd *(see Markers, page 60)*: 16 sc.

Rnd 3: (Sc in next sc, 2 sc in next sc) around: 24 sc.

Rnd 4: (Sc in next 2 sc, 2 sc in next sc) around: 32 sc.

Rnd 5: (Sc in next 3 sc, 2 sc in next sc) around: 40 sc.

Rnd 6: (Sc in next 4 sc, 2 sc in next sc) around: 48 sc.

Rnd 7: (Sc in next 5 sc, 2 sc in next sc) around: 56 sc.

Rnd 8: (Sc in next 6 sc, 2 sc in next sc) around: 64 sc.

Rnd 9: (Sc in next 7 sc, 2 sc in next sc) around: 72 sc.

Rnd 10: (Sc in next 8 sc, 2 sc in next sc) around: 80 sc.

Rnd 11: Sc in each sc around.

Rnd 12: (Sc in next 9 sc, 2 sc in next sc) around: 88 sc.

Rnd 13: Skip next sc, sc in next sc and in each sc around; slip st in next sc, finish off: 87 sc.

Rnd 14: With **right** side facing, join Cream with sc in same st as slip st; sc in each sc around; join with slip st to **both** loops of first sc, finish off.

Rnds 15-17: Repeat Rnds 16-18 of Front: 116 sc.

GUSSET

With Coral, ch 240.

Row 1 (Right side): Working in back ridge of beginning ch *(Fig. 1, page 60)*, sc in second ch from hook and in each ch across changing to Yellow in last sc *(Fig. 6b, page 61)*, cut Coral: 239 sc.

Note: Mark Row 1 as **right** side.

Row 2: Ch 1, turn; sc in first sc, (ch 1, skip next sc, sc in next sc) across changing to Violet in last sc, cut Yellow: 120 sc and 119 ch-1 sps.

Row 3: Ch 1, turn; sc in first sc and in next ch-1 sp, (ch 1, skip next sc, sc in next ch-1 sp) across to last sc, sc in last sc changing to Yellow, cut Violet: 122 sc and 117 ch-1 sp.

Row 4: Ch 1, turn; sc in first sc, (ch 1, skip next sc, sc in next ch-1 sp) across to last 2 sc, ch 1, skip next sc, sc in last sc changing to Violet, cut Yellow: 120 sc and 119 ch-1 sps.

Rows 5 and 6: Repeat Rows 3 and 4, changing to Coral at end of Row 6, cut Yellow: 120 sc and 119 ch-1 sps.

Row 7: Ch 1, turn; sc in each st and in each sp across; finish off leaving a long end for sewing: 239 sc.

FINISHING
JOINING

With **right** side of Gusset facing, being careful **not** to twist, and using long end, sew ends of rows together to form a ring.

With **right** sides of Gusset and Front facing, matching sts, and using Coral, sew through both pieces once to secure seam, leaving an ample yarn end to weave in later. Insert the needle from **right** to **left** through strands on one side *(Fig. A)*, then from **left** to **right** through strands on other side *(Fig. B)*. Continue in this manner, leaving 42 sc on Front unworked.

Fig. A

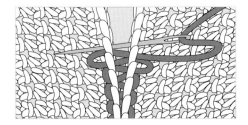

Fig. B

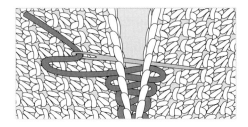

Repeat on opposite side of Gusset with Back, matching placement of Front and leaving 42 sc on Back unworked.

TASSEL (Make 2)

With Violet, make two tassels 5" (12.5 cm) long *(Figs. 12a & b, page 63)*, wrapping yarn around cardboard approximately 45 times. Tuck the long yarn ends at top of each tassel into the tassel. Trim the ends.

Join Violet with slip st around top yarn end on one tassel; work a 9" (23 cm) chain; slip st around top yarn end on remaining tassel.

Loop tassel chain around any stitch on Bag as desired.

Glue hook and loop fastener tape to **wrong** sides of opening.

MANDALA

 **EASY**

Finished Size: 10" (25.5 cm) diameter

SHOPPING LIST

Yarn (Medium Weight)

[3.5 ounces, 186 yards
(100 grams, 170 meters) per skein]:
- ☐ Aqua - 1 skein
- ☐ White - 1 skein
- ☐ Pink - 1 skein
- ☐ Rose - 1 skein
- ☐ Orange - 1 skein

Crochet Hook

- ☐ Size G (4 mm)
  or size needed for gauge

Additional Supplies

- ☐ 10" (25.5 cm) diameter metal ring

GAUGE INFORMATION

Gauge Swatch: 4⅝" (11.75 cm) diameter
Work same as Center through Rnd 6:
48 dc, 16 chs, and 8 sc.

STITCH GUIDE

TREBLE CROCHET (abbreviated tr)
YO twice, insert hook in st indicated, YO and pull up a loop (4 loops on hook),
(YO and draw through 2 loops on hook) 3 times.

DOUBLE TREBLE CROCHET (abbreviated dtr)
YO 3 times, insert hook in st indicated, YO and pull up a loop (5 loops on hook),
(YO and draw through 2 loops on hook) 4 times.

FRONT POST SINGLE CROCHET (abbreviated FPsc)
Insert hook from **front** to **back** around post of st indicated (**Fig. 5, page 61**), YO
and pull up a loop, YO and draw through both loops on hook.

FRONT POST DOUBLE CROCHET (abbreviated FPdc)
YO, insert hook from **front** to **back** around post of st indicated (**Fig. 5, page 61**),
YO and pull up a loop (3 loops on hook), (YO and draw through 2 loops on
hook) twice.

FRONT POST TREBLE CROCHET (abbreviated FPtr)
YO twice, insert hook from **front** to **back** around st indicated (**Fig. 5, page 61**),
YO and pull up a loop (4 loops on hook), (YO and draw through 2 loops on
hook) 3 times.

FRONT POST DOUBLE TREBLE CROCHET (abbreviated FPdtr)
YO 3 times, insert hook from **front** to **back** around st indicated (**Fig. 5, page 61**),
YO and pull up a loop (5 loops on hook), (YO and draw through 2 loops on
hook) 4 times.

PUFF STITCH (abbreviated Puff St) (uses one sc)
★ YO, insert hook in st indicated, YO and pull up a loop; repeat from ★ 2 times
more (7 loops on hook), YO and draw through all 7 loops on hook.

PICOT
Ch 2, slip st in top of dtr just made.

CENTER

Rnd 1 (Right side): With Aqua, ch 2, work 8 hdc in second ch from hook; join with slip st to first hdc.

Note: Loop a short piece of yarn around any stitch to mark Rnd 1 as **right** side.

Rnd 2: Ch 2 (**does not count as a st, now and throughout**), working in horizontal bar of each hdc (**Fig. 9, page 62**), 2 hdc in same st as joining and each hdc around; join with slip st to first hdc, finish off: 16 hdc.

Work Center with **right** side facing throughout.

Rnd 3: Join White with slip st in any hdc; (ch 4, dtr, work Picot, dtr, ch 4, slip st) in same st, ★ slip st in next 2 hdc, (ch 4, dtr, work Picot, dtr, ch 4, slip st) in same st as last slip st made; repeat from ★ around to last hdc, slip st in last hdc, place marker in last hdc worked into for st placement; join with slip st to joining slip st, finish off: 8 Picots.

Rnd 4: Join Orange with slip st in last Picot made on Rnd 3; ch 6, working **around** next slip st *(Fig. 8, page 62)*, slip st in marked hdc, remove marker, ch 6, ★ slip st in next Picot, ch 6, slip st **around** next slip st and in hdc on Rnd 2, ch 6; repeat from ★ around; join with slip st to joining slip st, finish off.

Rnd 5: Join Rose with slip st in Back Loop Only *(Fig. 3, page 60)* of same st as joining; ch 1, 2 sc in same st, slip st in top loops *(Fig. 2, page 60)* of first 4 chs of next ch-6 and last 4 chs of next ch-6, ★ 3 sc in Back Loop Only of next slip st, slip st in top loops of first 4 chs of next ch-6 and last 4 chs of next ch-6; repeat from ★ around, sc in same slip st as first sc; join with slip st to first sc, finish off: 64 slip sts and 24 sc.

Work in Back Loops Only through Rnd 14.

Rnd 6: Join Aqua with sc in same st as joining *(see Joining With Sc, page 60)*; ch 1, skip next sc and next 3 slip sts, 3 dc in each of next 2 slip sts, ch 1, skip next 3 slip sts and next sc, ★ sc in next sc, ch 1, skip next sc and next 3 slip sts, 3 dc in each of next 2 slip sts, ch 1, skip

next 3 slip sts and next sc; repeat from ★ around; join with slip st to first sc changing to White *(Fig. 6a, page 61)*, cut Aqua: 48 dc, 16 chs, and 8 sc.

Rnd 7: Ch 1, sc in same st as joining and in next 7 sts, 2 sc in next ch, (sc in next 8 sts, 2 sc in next ch) around; join with slip st to first sc changing to Pink, cut White: 80 sc.

Rnd 8: Ch 1, sc in each sc around; join with slip st to first sc, finish off.

Rnd 9: Skip first 3 sc and join Rose with sc in next sc; sc in next 4 sc, work FPtr around Back Loop Only of center sc on Rnd 5, ch 3, working **below** FPtr just made, work FPtr around same loop, skip next 5 sc from last sc made, ★ sc in next 5 sc, work FPtr around Back Loop Only of next center sc on Rnd 5, ch 3, working **below** FPtr just made, work FPtr around same loop, skip next 5 sc from last sc made; repeat from ★ around; join with slip st to first sc changing to White, cut Rose: 40 sc, 16 FPtr, and 8 ch-3 sps.

Rnd 10: Ch 1, sc in same st as joining and in next 4 sc, ★ † sc in next FPtr, working in **front** of next ch-3 *(Fig. 8, page 62)*,

(tr, ch 1, tr) in free loop of sc on Rnd 6 *(Fig. 4a, page 61)*, sc in next FPtr on Rnd 9 †, sc in next 5 sc; repeat from ★ 6 times **more**, then repeat from † to † once; join with slip st to first sc, finish off: 56 sc, 16 tr, and 8 ch-1 sps.

Rnd 11: Join Orange with sc in last tr; ★ † sc in next 7 sc and in next tr, working in **front** of next ch-1 and **between** tr, 2 dc in same loop as tr †, sc in next tr; repeat from ★ 6 times **more**, then repeat from † to † once; join with slip st to first sc, finish off: 72 sc and 16 dc.

Rnd 12: Join White with sc in same st as joining; sc in next 8 sc, work FPdc around next 2 tr on Rnd 10, skip next 2 dc, ★ sc in next 9 sc, work FPdc around next 2 tr on Rnd 10, skip next 2 dc; repeat from ★ around; join with slip st to first sc changing to Rose, cut White.

Rnd 13: Ch 1, 2 sc in same st, sc in next 8 sc, work FPdtr around next 2 FPtr on Rnd 9, skip next 2 FPdc on Rnd 12, ★ 2 sc in next sc, sc in next 8 sc, work FPdtr around next 2 FPtr on Rnd 9, skip next 2 FPdc on Rnd 12; repeat from ★ around; join with slip st to first sc, finish off: 80 sc and 16 FPdtr.

Rnd 14: Skip first sc and join Aqua with slip st in next sc; ch 2, work Puff St in same st, ch 2, ★ skip next st, work Puff St in next st, ch 2; repeat from ★ around to last sc, skip last sc; join with slip st to top of first Puff St, finish off: 48 Puff Sts and 48 ch-2 sps.

Rnd 15: Join White with slip st in both loops at top of first Puff St, working in **front** of next ch-2, dc in Back Loop Only of skipped sc **below**, ★ slip st in **both** loops at top of next Puff St, working in **front** of next ch-2, dc in Back Loop Only of skipped st **below**; repeat from ★ around; join with slip st to first slip st, finish off: 48 dc and 48 slip sts.

Rnd 16: Working in Back Loops Only, join Rose with sc in first dc; sc in next 10 sts, work FPtr around **both** posts of 2 FPdtr on Rnd 13, ★ sc in next 12 sts, work FPtr around **both** posts of 2 FPdtr on Rnd 13; repeat from ★ around to last slip st, work FPtr around **both** posts of last 2 FPdtr on Rnd 13, sc in last slip st; join with slip st to **both** loops of first sc, finish off: 104 sts.

Joining Rnd: Join Rose with sc around metal ring; work 25 sc, with **right** side of Center facing, work FPdc around any FPtr on Rnd 16, ★ work 26 sc around metal ring, work FPsc around next FPtr on Rnd 15; repeat from ★ around; join with slip st to first sc, finish off.

FINISHING
TASSEL (Make 3)
Make two Rose tassels and one Orange tassel, each 6" (15 cm) long, wrapping the yarn around the cardboard approximately 24 times *(Figs. 12a & b, page 63)*. Tuck the long yarn ends at top of each tassel into the tassel. Trim the ends.

JOINING
Center Tassel: With **right** side facing, join Orange with slip st in FPdc on Joining Rnd; ch 8, slip st around top yarn end on Orange Tassel; finish off.

Side Tassel: With **right** side facing, join Rose with slip st in tenth sc **before** Center Tassel; ch 15, slip st around top yarn end on one Rose Tassel; finish off.

Last Tassel: With **right** side facing, join Rose with slip st in tenth sc **after** Center Tassel, ch 15, slip st around top yarn end on last Rose Tassel; finish off.

Hanger: With **wrong** side facing, skip 2 FPsc from Center Tassel and join Orange with slip st around next FPsc; ch 80; skip next FPsc, slip st around next FPsc; finish off.

PILLOW

●●●○ INTERMEDIATE

Finished Size: 14" (35.5 cm) square

SHOPPING LIST

Yarn (Medium Weight)
[3.5 ounces, 186 yards
(100 grams, 170 meters) per skein]:
- ☐ Lilac - 3 skeins
- ☐ Green - 1 skein
- ☐ Dk Green - 1 skein
- ☐ Cream - 1 skein
- ☐ Gold - 1 skein

Crochet Hook
- ☐ Size G (4 mm)
  or size needed for gauge

Additional Supplies
- ☐ 14" (35.5 cm) square pillow form
- ☐ Yarn needle

GAUGE INFORMATION
In Back pattern,
  12 sts and 8 rows = 3" (7.5 cm)
Gauge Swatch: 3" (7.5 cm) diameter
Work same as Front on page 28 through
Rnd 4: 8 petals and 16 slip sts.

STITCH GUIDE

TREBLE CROCHET *(abbreviated tr)*
YO twice, insert hook in st or sp indicated, YO and pull up a loop (4 loops on hook), (YO and draw through 2 loops on hook) 3 times.

FRONT POST DOUBLE CROCHET *(abbreviated FPdc)*
YO, insert hook from **front** to **back** around post of st indicated *(Fig. 5, page 61)*, YO and pull up a loop (3 loops on hook), (YO and draw through 2 loops on hook) twice.

BACK POST DOUBLE CROCHET *(abbreviated BPdc)*
YO, insert hook from **back** to **front** around post of st indicated *(Fig. 5, page 61)*, YO and pull up a loop (3 loops on hook), (YO and draw through 2 loops on hook) twice.

BACK POST SINGLE CROCHET *(abbreviated BPsc)*
Insert hook from **back** to **front** around post of st indicated *(Fig. 5, page 61)*, YO and pull up a loop, YO and draw through both loops on hook.

BEGINNING CLUSTER (uses one st or sp)
Ch 2, ★ YO, insert hook in st or sp indicated, YO and pull up a loop, YO and draw through 2 loops on hook; repeat from ★ once **more**, YO and draw through all 3 loops on hook.

CLUSTER (uses one st or sp)
★ YO, insert hook in st or sp indicated, YO and pull up a loop, YO and draw through 2 loops on hook; repeat from ★ 2 times **more**, YO and draw through all 4 loops on hook.

FRONT

Rnd 1 (Right side): With Gold, ch 3, 16 dc in third ch from hook; join with slip st to first dc, finish off.

Note: Loop a short piece of yarn around any stitch to mark Rnd 1 as **right** side.

Work with **right** side facing throughout.

Rnd 2: Join Green with slip st in any dc, ch 2, dc in same st as joining and in next dc, ch 2, ★ slip st in same st and in next dc, ch 2, dc in same st and in next dc, ch 2; repeat from ★ around, slip st in same st as last dc; join with slip st to joining slip st, finish off: 8 petals and 16 slip sts.

Rnd 3: Working **around** slip sts *(Fig. 8, page 62)*, join Dk Green with sc around first slip st *(see Joining With Sc, page 60)*; ch 4, skip next slip st, ★ working **behind** petals, sc **around** next slip st, ch 4, skip next slip st; repeat from ★ around; join with slip st to first sc, do **not** finish off: 8 sc and 8 ch-4 sps.

Rnd 4: ★ Slip st in next ch-4 sp, (ch 2, 3 dc, ch 2, slip st) in same sp, skip next sc; repeat from ★ around; do **not** join, finish off: 8 petals and 16 slip sts.

Rnd 5: Working **behind** petals, join Lilac with sc in first slip st of any petal; ch 4, skip next slip st, ★ sc in next slip st, ch 4, skip next slip st; repeat from ★ around; join with slip st to first sc, do **not** finish off: 8 sc and 8 ch-4 sps.

Rnd 6: Ch 3 (**counts as first dc, now and throughout**), 5 dc in next ch-4 sp, (dc in next sc, 5 dc in next ch-4 sp) around; join with slip st to first dc changing to Cream *(Fig. 6a, page 61)*, cut Lilac: 48 dc.

Rnd 7: [Work Beginning Cluster, (ch 2, work Cluster) twice] in same st as joining, skip next 2 dc, slip st in next dc, place marker in slip st just made for st placement, ★ skip next 2 dc, in next dc work [Cluster, (ch 2, work Cluster) twice], skip next 2 dc, slip st in next dc; repeat from ★ around to last 2 dc, skip last 2 dc; join with slip st to top of Beginning Cluster, finish off: 24 Clusters, 16 ch-2 sps, and 8 slip sts.

Rnd 8: Join Dk Green with slip st **around** marked slip st; remove marker, ch 1, (work Cluster, ch 1) twice in each of next 2 ch-2 sps, ★ slip st **around** next slip st, ch 1, (work Cluster, ch 1) twice in each of next 2 ch-2 sps; repeat from ★ around; join with slip st to joining slip st, finish off: 32 Clusters, 32 ch-1 sps, and 8 slip sts.

Rnd 9: Join Gold with sc in any slip st; working **behind** previous rnds, ch 8, (sc in next slip st, ch 8) around; join with slip st to first sc, finish off: 8 sc and 8 ch-8 sps.

Rnd 10: Join Cream with dc in any ch-8 sp *(see Joining With Dc, page 60)*; 5 dc in same sp, ★ † holding **same** ch-8 sp behind Rnd 8 and working through **both** sps, work (Cluster, ch 3, Cluster) in center ch-1 sp on Rnd 8, 6 dc in **same** ch-8 sp, 5 dc in next ch-8 sp, working **around same** ch-8 sp and **behind** previous rnds, dc in top of center Cluster on Rnd 7 †, 6 dc in **same** ch-8 sp and in next ch-8 sp; repeat from ★ 2 times **more**, then repeat from † to † once, place marker in last dc made for st placement, 6 dc in **same** ch-8 sp as last dc; join with slip st to first dc, finish off: 96 dc, 8 Clusters, and 4 ch-3 sps.

Rnd 11: Holding center ch-1 sp on Rnd 8 in **front** of marked dc and working through **both** layers, join Lilac with slip st in marked dc; remove marker; ch 4 **(counts as first tr)**, 7 tr in same st, ★ † ch 5, working **behind** previous rnds, slip st in top of center Cluster on Rnd 7, ch 5 †, skip next 11 dc on Rnd 10, holding next center ch-1 sp on Rnd 8 in **front** of next dc and working through **both** layers, 8 tr in dc; repeat from ★ 2 times **more**, then repeat from † to † once; join with slip st to first tr, finish off: 32 tr and 8 ch-5 sps.

Rnd 12: Join Green with dc in first ch-5 sp; 5 dc in same sp, skip next slip st, 6 dc in next ch-5 sp, skip next tr, work Cluster in sp **before** next tr *(Fig. 7, page 62)*, (ch 1, work Cluster in sp **before** next tr) 6 times, place marker in fourth Cluster made for st placement, ★ (6 dc in next ch-5 sp, skip next st) twice, work Cluster in sp **before** next tr, (ch 1, work Cluster in sp **before** next tr) 6 times; repeat from ★ 2 times **more**; join with slip st to first dc, finish off: 48 dc, 28 Clusters, and 24 ch-1 sps.

29

Rnd 13: Join Cream with dc in marked Cluster, remove marker; ch 3, dc in same st, ★ † (dc in next ch-1 sp and in next Cluster) 3 times, dc in next 12 dc, (dc in next Cluster and in next ch-1 sp) 3 times †, (dc, ch 3, dc) in next Cluster; repeat from ★ 2 times **more**, then repeat from † to † once; join with slip st to first dc, finish off: 104 dc and 4 corner ch-3 sps.

Rnd 14: Holding Rnd 10 in **front** of Rnd 13, skip 13 dc from corner ch-3 sp and join Gold with slip st in ch-3 sp on Rnd 10 and in sp **before** next dc working through **both** layers; work [Beginning Cluster, (ch 1, work Cluster) twice] in same sp, ch 8, ★ † working **behind** previous rnds, skip next sc on Rnd 9, slip st around ch-8 (**below** corner 7-tr group on Rnd 11), ch 8 †, working through **both** layers of next ch-3 sp on Rnd 10 and sp **before** 14th dc from corner ch-3 sp on Rnd 13, work [Cluster, (ch 1, work Cluster) twice] in next sp, ch 8; repeat from ★ 2 times **more**, then repeat from † to † once, place marker around last ch-8 made for st placement; join with slip st to top of Beginning Cluster, finish off: 12 Clusters, 8 ch-1 sps, and 8 ch-8 sps.

Rnd 15: Join Dk Green with sc in first dc of any corner group on Rnd 13; ★ † working in **front** of corner ch-3, work (Cluster, ch 1, Cluster) in corner Cluster on Rnd 12 **below**, sc in next 10 dc, ch 3, skip next 3 dc, working **behind** next ch-8, slip st in back of center Cluster on Rnd 14, ch 3, working **behind** next ch-8, skip next 3 dc on Rnd 12 †, sc in next 10 dc; repeat from ★ 2 times **more**, then repeat from † to † once, sc in last 9 dc; join with slip st to first sc, finish off: 80 sc, 8 Clusters, and 4 corner ch-1 sps.

Rnd 16: Join Lilac with slip st in marked ch-8 sp **before** first Cluster on Rnd 14, remove marker, work (Beginning Cluster, ch 1, Cluster) in same sp, ★ † ch 1, (work Cluster, ch 1) twice in each of next 2 ch-1 sps, work (Cluster, ch 1, Cluster) in next ch-8 sp, ch 8, working **behind** previous rnds, slip st in loops at bottom of tr on Rnd 11, ch 8 †, work (Cluster, ch 1, Cluster) in ch-8 sp **before** next Cluster on Rnd 14; repeat from ★ 2 times **more**, then repeat from † to † once; join with slip st to top of Beginning Cluster, finish off: 32 Clusters and 28 ch-1 sps.

Rnd 17: Holding sc on Rnd 15 in **front** of Beginning Cluster, and working through **both** sts, join Cream with dc in 7th sc from corner on Rnd 15; 6 dc in same st, ★ † ch 4, working **behind** next 3 Clusters, slip st in back of next Cluster, ch 4, skip next 2 Clusters and next 3 sc on Rnd 15, holding next sc in **front** of next Cluster and working through **both** sts, 7 dc in next st, ch 4, working **behind** previous rnds, slip st in skipped corner ch-3 sp on Rnd 13, ch 4 †, skip next 6 sc from second corner Cluster on Rnd 15, holding next sc in **front** of first Cluster of next 8-Cluster group and working through **both** sts, 7 dc in next st; repeat from ★ 2 times **more**, then repeat from † to † once; join with slip st to first dc, finish off: 56 dc and 16 ch-4 sps.

Rnd 18: Join Green with slip st in any corner ch-1 sp on Rnd 15; work (Beginning Cluster, ch 1, Cluster, ch 3, Cluster, ch 1, Cluster) in same sp, ★ † dc in next 4 sc on same rnd, working **around** ch-4 on Rnd 17, dc in next sc, ch 1, skip next 3 dc, work BPsc around next dc, ch 1, skip next ch-1 sp on Rnd 16, working **around** ch-4 on Rnd 17, 2 dc in next ch-1 sp, 2 sc in each of next 3 ch-1 sps on Rnd 16, working **around** ch-4 on Rnd 17, 2 dc in next ch-1 sp on Rnd 16, ch 1, skip next 3 dc on Rnd 17, work BPsc around next dc, ch 1, skip next sc on Rnd 15, working **around** ch-4

on Rnd 17, dc in next sc, working in sc **only**, dc in next 4 sc †, work (Cluster, ch 1, Cluster, ch 3, Cluster, ch 1, Cluster) in next corner ch-1 sp on Rnd 15; repeat from ★ 2 times **more**, then repeat from † to † once; join with slip st to top of Beginning Cluster, finish off: 104 sts and 28 sps.

Rnd 19: Join Cream with dc in any corner ch-3 sp; 4 dc in same sp, ★ † dc in next Cluster and in next ch-1 sp, dc in next 6 sts, hdc in next ch-1 sp, hdc in next BPsc and in next ch-1 sp, sc in next 10 sts, hdc in next ch-1 sp, hdc in next BPsc and in next ch-1 sp, dc in next 6 sts, dc in next

ch-1 sp and in next Cluster †, 5 dc in next ch-3 sp; repeat from ★ 2 times **more**, then repeat from † to † once; join with slip st to first dc, finish off: 148 sts.

Rnd 20: Join Gold with slip st in center dc of any corner 5-dc group; ch 2 (**does not count as a st, now and throughout**), 5 hdc in same st, hdc in each st across to center dc of next corner 5-dc group, ★ 5 hdc in center dc, hdc in each st across to center dc of next corner 5-dc group; repeat from ★ around; join with slip st to first hdc, finish off: 164 hdc.

Rnd 21: Working in horizontal bar of each hdc *(Fig. 9, page 62)*, join Green with slip st in center hdc of any corner 5-hdc group; ch 2, 5 hdc in same st, hdc in next hdc and in each hdc around working 5 hdc in center hdc of each corner 5-hdc group; join with slip st to first hdc, finish off: 180 hdc.

Rnd 22: With Dk Green, repeat Rnd 21: 196 hdc.

Rnd 23: With Lilac, repeat Rnd 21: 212 hdc.

Rnd 24: With Cream, repeat Rnd 21: 228 hdc.

Rnd 25: Working in horizontal bar of each hdc, join Green with dc in center hdc of any corner 5-hdc group; 4 dc in same st, ★ † work Cluster in next hdc, (ch 1, skip next hdc, work Cluster in next hdc) across to within one hdc of center hdc of next corner 5-hdc group, skip next hdc †, 5 dc in center hdc; repeat from ★ 2 times **more**, then repeat from † to † once; join with slip st to **both** loops of first dc, do **not** finish off: 240 sts.

Rnd 26: Ch 1, working in both loops, sc in same st and in next dc, 5 sc in next dc, sc in next st and in each ch around working 5 sc in center dc of each corner 5-dc group; join with slip st to first sc, finish off: 256 sc.

BACK

With Lilac, ch 59; place marker in third ch from hook for st placement.

Row 1: Dc in fourth ch from hook and in each ch across **(3 skipped chs count as first dc)**: 57 dc.

Row 2 (Right side): Ch 3, turn; work FPdc around next 2 dc, (work BPdc around next 3 dc, work FPdc around next 3 dc) across.

Note: Mark Row 2 as **right** side.

Rows 3-39: Ch 3, turn; work FPdc around next 2 sts, (work BPdc around next 3 sts, work FPdc around next 3 sts) across.

Trim: Ch 1, turn; 5 sc in first st, work 59 sc across to last st, 5 sc in last st; work 59 sc evenly spaced across ends of rows; working in free loops of beginning ch *(Fig. 4b, page 61)*, 5 sc in marked ch, remove marker, work 59 sc across to last ch, 5 sc in last ch; work 59 sc evenly spaced across ends of rows; join with slip st to first sc, finish off: 256 sc.

With **wrong** sides together, using Green, and working through **both** loops of each sc, sew Front and Back together, inserting pillow form before closing.

POUF

●●○○ EASY

Finished Size:
Approximately 65" diameter x 13" high
(165 cm x 33 cm)

SHOPPING LIST

Yarn (Medium Weight)
[1.75 ounces, 80 yards
(50 grams, 73 meters) per skein]:
☐ Cream - 4 skeins
☐ Violet - 3 skeins
☐ Dk Violet - 3 skeins
☐ Tan - 3 skeins

Crochet Hook
☐ Size H (5 mm)
   or size needed for gauge

Additional Supplies
☐ Polyester fiberfill - 50 ounces
   (1,420 grams)
☐ Safety pin
☐ Yarn needle

GAUGE INFORMATION
Gauge Swatch: 4" (10 cm) diameter
Work same as Pouf on page 36 through
Rnd 4 : 48 sts.

STITCH GUIDE

DOUBLE CROCHET 2 TOGETHER *(abbreviated dc2tog)* (uses next 2 sts)

★ YO, insert hook in **next** st, YO and pull up a loop, YO and draw through 2 loops on hook; repeat from ★ once **more**, YO and draw through all 3 loops on hook (**counts as one dc**).

SINGLE CROCHET 2 TOGETHER *(abbreviated sc2tog)*

Pull up a loop in next 2 sts, YO and draw through all 3 loops on hook (**counts as one sc**).

SPLIT FRONT POST TREBLE CROCHET *(abbreviated split FPtr)* (uses 2 FPtr)

YO twice, insert hook from **front** to **back** around post of FPtr **below** next dc *(Fig. 5, page 61)*, YO and pull up a loop (4 loops on hook), (YO and draw through 2 loops on hook) twice (2 loops on hook), YO twice, insert hook from **front** to **back** around post of **next** FPtr, YO and pull up a loop, (YO and draw through 2 loops on hook) twice, YO and draw through all 3 loops on hook (**counts as one st**).

FRONT POST TREBLE CROCHET *(abbreviated FPtr)*

YO twice, insert hook from **front** to **back** around post of st indicated *(Fig. 5, page 61)*, YO and pull up a loop (4 loops on hook), (YO and draw through 2 loops on hook) 3 times. Skip dc **behind** FPtr.

FRONT POST DOUBLE CROCHET *(abbreviated FPdc)*

YO, insert hook from **front** to **back** around post of st indicated *(Fig. 5, page 61)*, YO and pull up a loop (3 loops on hook), (YO and draw through 2 loops on hook) twice. Skip dc **behind** FPdc.

CROSS ST (uses one split FPtr)

Skip first leg of split FPtr **below** next dc, work FPtr around next leg, working in **front** of FPtr just made, work FPtr around skipped leg. Skip dc **behind** Cross St.

POUF

Rnd 1 (Right side)**:** With Dk Violet, ch 4, 11 dc in fourth ch from hook **(3 skipped chs count as first dc)**; join with slip st to first dc changing to Cream *(Fig. 6a, page 61)*, cut Dk Violet: 12 dc.

Note: Loop a short piece of yarn around any stitch to mark Rnd 1 as **right** side.

Rnd 2: Ch 1, 2 sc in same st as joining, work 2 FPdc around next dc, ★ 2 sc in next dc, work 2 FPdc around next dc; repeat from ★ around; join with slip st to first sc changing to Violet, cut Cream: 24 sts.

Rnd 3: Ch 3 **(counts as first dc, now and throughout)**, 2 dc in next sc, (dc in next st, 2 dc in next st) around; join with slip st to first dc, finish off: 36 dc.

Rnd 4: With **right** side facing, skip first dc and join Cream with sc in next dc *(see Joining With Sc, page 60)*; 2 sc in next dc, work FPtr around FPdc **below** next dc, ★ sc in next dc, 2 sc in next dc, work FPtr around FPdc **below** next dc; repeat from ★ around; join with slip st to first sc changing to Tan, cut Cream: 48 sts.

Rnd 5: Ch 3, dc in next 2 sc, 2 dc in next FPtr, (dc in next 3 sc, 2 dc in next FPtr) around; join with slip st to first dc changing to Cream, cut Tan: 60 dc.

Rnd 6: Ch 1, sc in same st as joining, ★ † work 2 FPdc around sc **below** next dc, sc in next dc, work FPtr around FPtr **below** next dc, sc in next 4 dc, work FPtr around FPtr **below** next dc †, sc in next dc; repeat from ★ 4 times **more**, then repeat from † to † once; join with slip st

to first sc changing to Dk Violet, cut Cream: 12 FPdc, 12 FPtr, and 36 sc.

Rnd 7: Ch 3, dc in next st and in each st around; join with slip st to first dc, finish off.

Rnd 8: With **right** side facing, skip first 2 dc and join Cream with sc in next dc; ★ † work FPtr around FPdc **below** next dc, sc in next 2 dc, work FPtr around FPtr **below** next dc, sc in next dc, work FPtr around FPtr **below** next dc, sc in next 2 dc, work FPtr around FPdc **below** next dc †, sc in next dc; repeat from ★ 4 times **more**, then repeat from † to † once; join with slip st to first sc changing to Violet, cut Cream.

Rnd 9: Ch 3, dc in next 3 sts, 2 dc in next st, (dc in next 4 sts, 2 dc in next st) around; join with slip st to first dc, finish off: 72 dc.

Rnd 10: With **right** side facing, skip first 3 dc and join Cream with sc in next dc; sc in next 3 dc, ★ † work split FPtr, do **not** skip dc behind split FPtr, sc in next 4 dc, work FPtr around FPtr **below** next dc, sc in next 2 dc, work FPtr around FPtr **below** next dc †, sc in next 4 dc; repeat from ★ 4 times **more**, then repeat from † to † once; join with slip st to first sc changing to Tan, cut Cream: 78 sts.

Rnd 11: Ch 3, dc in next sc and in each st around; join with slip st to first dc, finish off.

Rnd 12: With **right** side facing, skip first dc and join Cream with sc in next dc; sc in next 2 dc, ★ † work Cross St, sc in next 4 dc, work FPtr around FPtr **below** next dc, sc in next 3 dc, work FPtr around FPtr **below** next dc †, sc in next 3 dc; repeat from ★ 4 times **more**, then repeat from † to † once; join with slip st to first sc changing to Dk Violet, cut Cream: 84 sts.

Rnd 13: Ch 3, dc in next 4 sts, 2 dc in next st, (dc in next 13 sts, 2 dc in next st) around to last 9 sts, dc in last 9 sts; join with slip st to first dc changing to Cream, cut Dk Violet: 90 dc.

Rnd 14: Ch 1, sc in same st as joining and in next 2 dc, ★ † work FPtr around next FPtr **below** next dc, sc in next 2 dc, work FPtr around next FPtr **below** next dc, sc in next 5 dc, work FPtr around next 2 FPtr **below** next 2 dc †, sc in next 4 dc; repeat from ★ 4 times **more**, repeat from † to † once, sc in last dc; join with slip st to first sc, finish off: 24 FPtr and 66 sc.

Rnd 15: With **right** side facing, join Violet with dc in last sc made; dc in next 13 sts, 2 dc in next st, (dc in next 14 sts, 2 dc in next st) around; join with slip st to first dc changing to Cream, cut Violet: 96 dc.

Rnd 16: Ch 1, sc in same st as joining and in next 5 dc, ★ † work split FPtr, skip dc **behind** split FPtr, sc in next 7 dc, skip next FPtr **below** next dc, work FPtr around next FPtr, working in **front** of FPtr just made, work FPtr around skipped FPtr †, sc in next 6 dc; repeat from ★ 4 times **more**, then repeat from † to † once; join with slip st to first sc changing to Tan, cut Cream: 78 sc, 12 FPtr, and 6 split FPtr.

Rnd 17: Ch 3, dc in next 14 sts, 2 dc in next st, (dc in next 15 sts, 2 dc in next st) around; join with slip st to first dc, finish off: 102 dc.

Rnd 18: With **right** side facing, skip first dc and join Cream with sc in next dc; sc in next dc, ★ † 2 sc in next dc, sc in next 2 dc, work FPtr around split FPtr **below** next dc, sc in next 7 dc, work FPtr around next FPtr **below** next dc, sc in next 2 dc, work FPtr around next FPtr **below** next dc †, sc in next 2 dc; repeat from ★ 4 times **more**, then repeat from † to † once; join with slip st to first sc changing to Dk Violet, cut Cream: 108 sts.

Rnd 19: Ch 3, dc in next 2 sc, 2 dc in next sc, dc in next 6 sts, 2 dc in next st, ★ dc in next 10 sts, 2 dc in next st, dc in next 6 sts, 2 dc in next st; repeat from ★ around to last 7 sts, dc in last 7 sts; join with slip st to first dc changing to Cream, cut Dk Violet: 120 dc.

Rnd 20: Ch 1, sc in same st as joining and in next 4 dc, ★ † 2 sc in next dc, sc in next 7 dc, 2 sc in next dc, sc in next 5 dc, work split FPtr, skip dc **behind** split FPtr †, sc in next 5 dc; repeat from ★ 4 times **more**, then repeat from † to † once; join with slip st to first sc changing to Violet, cut Cream: 132 sts.

Rnd 21: Ch 3, dc in next 5 sts, 2 dc in next st, dc in next 8 sts, 2 dc in next st, ★ dc in next 12 sts, 2 dc in next st, dc in next 8 sts, 2 dc in next st; repeat from ★ around to last 6 sts, dc in last 6 sts; join with slip st to first dc changing to Cream, cut Violet: 144 dc.

Rnd 22: Ch 1, sc in same st as joining and in next 6 dc, ★ † 2 sc in next dc, sc in next 9 dc, 2 sc in next dc, sc in next 5 dc, work FPtr around split FPtr **below** next dc †, sc in next 7 dc; repeat from ★ 4 times **more**, then repeat from † to † once; join with slip st to first sc changing to Tan, cut Cream: 156 sts.

Rnd 23: Ch 3, dc in next 24 sts, 2 dc in next st, (dc in next 25 sts, 2 dc in next st) around; join with slip st to first dc changing to Cream, cut Tan: 162 dc.

Rnd 24: Ch 1, sc in same st as joining and in next 25 dc, 2 sc in next dc, (sc in next 26 dc, 2 sc in next dc) around; join with slip st to first sc changing to Dk Violet, cut Cream: 168 sc.

Rnd 25: Ch 3, dc in next 26 sc, 2 dc in next sc, (dc in next 27 sc, 2 dc in next sc) around; join with slip st to first dc changing to Cream, cut Dk Violet: 174 dc.

Rnd 26: Ch 1, sc in same st as joining and in each dc around; join with slip st to first sc changing to Violet, cut Cream.

Rnd 27: Ch 3, dc in next sc and in each sc around; join with slip st to first dc changing to Cream, cut Violet.

Rnd 28: Ch 1, sc in same st as joining and in each dc around; join with slip st to first sc changing to Tan, cut Cream.

Rnd 29: Ch 3, dc in next sc and in each sc around; join with slip st to first dc changing to Cream, cut Tan.

Rnd 30: Ch 1, sc in same st as joining and in next 2 dc, work FPtr around sc **below** next dc, ★ sc in next 5 dc, work FPtr around sc **below** next dc; repeat from ★ around to last 2 dc, sc in last 2 dc; join with slip st to first sc changing to Dk Violet, cut Cream.

Rnd 31: Ch 3, dc in next sc and in each st around; join with slip st to first dc changing to Cream, cut Dk Violet.

Rnd 32: Ch 1, sc in same st as joining, ★ † work FPtr around next FPtr **below** next dc, sc in next 3 dc, work FPtr **below** same FPtr as last FPtr made †, sc in next dc; repeat from ★ around to last 5 sts, then repeat from † to † once; join with slip st to first sc changing to Violet, cut Cream.

Rnd 33: Ch 3, dc in next st and in each st around; join with slip st to first dc changing to Cream, cut Violet.

Rnd 34: Ch 1, sc in same st as joining and in next 2 dc, work split FPtr, skip dc **behind** split FPtr, ★ sc in next 5 dc, work split FPtr, skip dc **behind** split FPtr; repeat from ★ around to last 2 dc, sc in last 2 sc; join with slip st to first sc changing to Tan, cut Cream.

Rnd 35: Ch 3, dc in next st and in each st around; join with slip st to first dc, finish off.

Rnd 36: With **right** side facing, skip first dc and join Cream with sc in next dc; sc in next dc, ★ † work FPtr around next split FPtr, sc in next 2 dc, work FPtr around sc **below** next dc †, sc in next 2 dc; repeat from ★ around to last 4 dc, then repeat from † to † once; join with slip st to first sc changing to Dk Violet, cut Cream.

Rnd 37: Ch 3, dc in next sc and in each st around; join with slip st to first dc, finish off.

Rnd 38: With **right** side facing, skip first 2 dc and join Cream with sc in next dc; ★ † work FPtr around next FPtr, sc in next 3 dc, work FPtr **below** same FPtr as last FPtr made †, sc in next dc; repeat from ★ around to last 5 dc, then repeat from † to † once; join with slip st to first sc changing to Violet, cut Cream.

Rnds 39-47: Repeat Rnds 33-38 once, then repeat Rnds 33-35 once **more**.

Rnd 48: With **right** side facing, skip first 4 dc and join Cream with sc in next dc; sc in next 4 dc, work FPtr around next split FPtr, ★ sc in next 5 dc, work FPtr around next split FPtr; repeat from ★ around; join with slip st to first sc changing to Dk Violet, cut Cream.

Rnd 49: Ch 3, dc in next sc and in each st around; join with slip st to first dc changing to Cream, cut Dk Violet.

Rnds 50-52: Repeat Rnds 26-28.

Rnd 53: Ch 3, dc in next 26 sc, dc2tog, (dc in next 27 sc, dc2tog) around; join with slip st to first dc changing to Cream, cut Tan: 168 dc.

Rnd 54: Ch 1, sc in same st as joining and in next 25 dc, sc2tog, (sc in next 26 dc, sc2tog) around; join with slip st to first sc changing to Dk Violet, cut Cream: 162 sc.

Rnd 55: Ch 3, dc in next 24 sc, dc2tog, (dc in next 25 sc, dc2tog) around; join with slip st to first dc changing to Cream, cut Dk Violet: 156 dc.

Rnd 56: Ch 1, sc in same st as joining and in next 10 dc, sc2tog, (sc in next 11 dc, sc2tog) around; join with slip st to first sc changing to Violet, cut Cream: 144 sc.

Rnd 57: Ch 3, dc in next 9 sc, dc2tog, (dc in next 10 sc, dc2tog) around; join with slip st to first dc changing to Cream, cut Violet: 132 dc.

Rnd 58: Ch 1, sc in same st as joining and in next 8 dc, sc2tog, (sc in next 9 dc, sc2tog) around; join with slip st to first sc changing to Tan, cut Cream: 120 sc.

Rnd 59: Ch 3, dc in next 7 sc, dc2tog, (dc in next 8 sc, dc2tog) around; join with slip st to first dc changing Cream, cut Tan: 108 dc.

Rnd 60: Ch 1, sc in same st as joining and in next 15 dc, sc2tog, (sc in next 16 dc, sc2tog) around; join with slip st to first sc changing to Dk Violet, cut Cream: 102 sc.

Rnd 61: Ch 3, dc in next 14 sc, dc2tog, (dc in next 15 sc, dc2tog) around; join with slip st to first dc changing to Cream, cut Dk Violet: 96 dc.

Rnd 62: Ch 1, sc in same st as joining and in each dc around; join with slip st to first sc changing to Violet, cut Cream.

Rnd 63: Ch 3, dc in next 13 sc, dc2tog, (dc in next 14 sc, dc2tog) around; join with slip st to first dc changing to Cream, cut Violet: 90 dc.

Rnd 64: Ch 1, sc in same st as joining and in each dc around, join with slip st to first sc changing to Tan, cut Cream.

Rnd 65: Ch 3, dc in next 12 sc, dc2tog, (dc in next 13 sc, dc2tog) around; join with slip st to first dc changing to Cream, cut Tan: 84 dc.

Rnd 66: Ch 1, sc in same st as joining and in next 11 dc, sc2tog, (sc in next 12 dc, sc2tog) around; join with slip st to first sc changing to Dk Violet, cut Cream: 78 sc.

Rnd 67: Ch 3, dc in next sc and in each sc around; join with slip st to first dc changing to Cream, cut Dk Violet.

Rnd 68: Ch 1, sc in same st as joining and next 10 dc, sc2tog, (sc in next 11 dc, sc2tog) around; join with slip st to first sc changing to Violet, cut Cream: 72 sc.

Rnd 69: Ch 3, dc in next 3 sc, dc2tog, (dc in next 4 sc, dc2tog) around; join with slip st to first dc changing to Cream, cut Violet, place loop from hook onto safety pin to keep piece from unraveling: 60 dc.

Stuff Pouf firmly with polyester fiberfill.

Rnd 70: Remove loop from safety pin and place on hook; ch 1, sc in same st as joining and in next 2 dc, sc2tog, (sc in next 3 dc, sc2tog) around; join with slip st to first sc changing to Tan, cut Cream: 48 sc.

Rnd 71: Ch 3, dc in next sc, dc2tog, (dc in next 2 sc, dc2tog) around; join with slip st to first dc changing to Cream, cut Tan: 36 dc.

Rnd 72: Ch 1, sc in same st as joining, sc2tog, (sc in next dc, sc2tog) around; join with slip st to first sc changing to Dk Violet, cut Cream: 24 sc.

Rnd 73: Ch 2 **(does not count as a st)**, dc2tog around; join with slip st to first dc changing to Cream, cut Dk Violet: 12 dc.

Rnd 74: Ch 1, sc2tog around; join with slip st to first sc, finish off leaving a long end for sewing: 6 sc.

Thread yarn needle with long end and weave through sts on Rnd 74 to close.

DOILY RUG

●●○○ EASY

Finished Size: 25" (63.5 cm) diameter

SHOPPING LIST

Yarn (Medium Weight)
[2.5 ounces, 120 yards
(70.9 grams, 109 meters) per skein]:
☐ Yellow - 1 skein
☐ Aqua - 1 skein
☐ Dk Orange - 1 skein
☐ Lime - 1 skein
☐ Cream - 1 skein

Crochet Hook
☐ Size H (5 mm)
   or size needed for gauge

GAUGE INFORMATION
14 dc and 8 rows = 4" (10 cm)
Gauge Swatch: 6" (15 cm) diameter
Work same as Body on page 44 through
Rnd 7: 56 sts.

STITCH GUIDE

TREBLE CROCHET *(abbreviated tr)*
YO twice, insert hook in st or sp indicated, YO and pull up a loop (4 loops on hook), (YO and draw through 2 loops on hook) 3 times.

BOBBLE (uses one st)
★ YO, insert hook in st indicated, YO and pull up loop, YO and draw through 2 loops on hook; repeat from ★ 4 times **more**, YO and draw through all 6 loops on hook.

BEGINNING CLUSTER (uses one st)
Ch 2, ★ YO, insert hook in st indicated, YO and pull up loop, YO and draw through 2 loops on hook; repeat from ★ once **more**, YO and draw through all 3 loops on hook.

CLUSTER (uses one st)
★ YO, insert hook in st indicated, YO and pull up loop, YO and draw through 2 loops on hook; repeat from ★ 2 times **more**, YO and draw through all 4 loops on hook.

SPLIT FRONT POST DOUBLE TREBLE CROCHET *(abbreviated split FPdtr)*
  (uses 2 FPtr)
YO 3 times, insert hook from **front** to **back** around post of FPtr **below** *(Fig. 5, page 61)*, YO and pull up a loop (5 loops on hook), (YO and draw through 2 loops on hook) 3 times, YO 3 times, insert hook from **front** to **back** around post of next FPtr **below**, (YO and draw through 2 loops on hook) 3 times, YO and draw through all 3 loops on hook.

FRONT POST TREBLE CROCHET *(abbreviated FPtr)*
YO twice, insert hook from **front** to **back** around post of st indicated *(Fig. 5, page 61)*, YO and pull up a loop (4 loops on hook), (YO and draw through 2 loops on hook) 3 times.

FRONT POST DOUBLE CROCHET *(abbreviated FPdc)*
YO, insert hook from **front** to **back** around post of st indicated *(Fig. 5, page 61)*, YO and pull up a loop (3 loops on hook), (YO and draw through 2 loops on hook) twice.

BACK POST SINGLE CROCHET *(abbreviated BPsc)*
Insert hook from **back** to **front** around post of st indicated *(Fig. 5, page 61)*, YO and pull up a loop, YO and draw through both loops on hook.

PICOT
Ch 3, slip st in st indicated.

Work with **right** side facing throughout.

BODY

Rnd 1 (Right side)**:** With Cream, ch 2, 8 sc in second ch from hook; join with slip st to first sc changing to Yellow *(Fig. 6a, page 61)*, cut Cream.

Note: Loop a short piece of yarn around any stitch to mark Rnd 1 as **right** side.

Rnd 2: Work Beginning Cluster in same st as joining, ch 1, (work Cluster in next sc, ch 1) around; join with slip st to top of Beginning Cluster, finish off: 8 Clusters and 8 ch-1 sps.

Rnd 3: Join Aqua with dc in any ch-1 sp *(see Joining With Dc, page 60)*; (dc, ch 1, 2 dc) in same sp, (2 dc, ch 1, 2 dc) in next ch-1 sp and in each ch-1 sp around; join with slip st to first dc, finish off: 32 dc and 8 ch-1 sps.

Rnd 4: Join Dk Orange with dc in any ch-1 sp; 6 dc in same sp, skip next 2 dc, slip st in sp **before** next dc *(Fig. 7, page 62)*, ★ skip next 2 dc, 7 dc in next ch-1 sp, skip next 2 dc, slip st in sp **before** next dc; repeat from ★ around; join with slip st to first dc, finish off: 64 sts.

Rnd 5: Working **around** slip sts on Rnd 4 *(Fig. 8, page 62)*, join Lime with sc **around** any slip st *(see Joining With Sc, page 60)*; sc in Back Loops Only of next 4 dc *(Fig. 3, page 60)*, place marker around last sc made for st placement, sc in Back Loops Only of next 3 dc, ★ sc **around** next slip st, sc in Back Loops Only of next 7 dc; repeat from ★ around; join with slip st to **both** loops of first sc, finish off.

Rnd 6: Join Yellow with sc in marked sc; remove marker, ch 3, skip next 3 sc, work Bobble in next sc, ch 3, ★ skip next 3 sc, sc in next sc, ch 3, skip next 3 sc, work Bobble in next sc, ch 3; repeat from ★ around; join with slip st to first sc, finish off: 8 Bobbles, 8 sc, and 16 ch-3 sps.

Rnd 7: Working around previous rnd, join Aqua with sc **around** first sc; working **around** next ch-3 and in Back Loops Only of skipped sc **below**, ★ † hdc in next sc, dc in next sc, tr in next sc, skip next Bobble, tr in next sc, dc in next sc, hdc in next sc †, sc **around** next sc; repeat from ★ 6 times **more**, then repeat from † to † once; join with slip st to first sc, finish off: 56 sts.

Rnd 8: Working in Back Loops Only, skip first 4 sts and join Cream with sc in next tr; sc in next 2 sts, 2 sc in next sc, (sc in next 6 sts, 2 sc in next sc) around to last 3 sts, sc in last 3 sts; join with slip st to first sc changing to Lime, cut Cream: 64 sc.

Rnd 9: Working in Back Loops Only, ch 3 **(counts as first dc, now and throughout)**, dc in next 4 sc, 2 dc in next sc, (dc in next 7 sc, 2 dc in next sc) around to last 2 sc, dc in last 2 sc; join with slip st to first dc, finish off: 72 dc.

Rnd 10: Working in Back Loops Only, join Cream with sc in second dc of any 2-dc group; sc in same st and in next 8 dc, (2 sc in next dc, sc in next 8 dc) around; join with slip st to first sc, finish off: 80 sc.

Rnd 11: Working in Back Loops Only, join Aqua with dc in second sc of any 2-sc group; dc in same st and in next 2 sc, place marker in last dc made for st placement, dc in next 7 sc, (2 dc in next sc, dc in next 9 sc) around; join with slip st to **both** loops of first dc, finish off: 88 dc.

Rnd 12: Working in both loops, skip first dc and join Yellow with dc in next dc; 2 dc in same st, ch 3, skip next 3 dc, (3 dc in next dc, ch 3, skip next 3 dc) around; join with slip st to first dc, finish off: 66 dc and 22 ch-3 sps.

Rnd 13: Working **around** ch-3, Join Cream with dc in marked dc on Rnd 11; (dc, ch 1, 2 dc) in same st, remove marker, skip next dc on Rnd 12, slip st in next dc, ★ working **around** next ch-3, (2 dc, ch 1, 2 dc) in center dc of next skipped 3-dc group on Rnd 11, skip next dc on Rnd 12, slip st in next dc; repeat from ★ around; join with slip st to first dc, finish off: 22 ch-1 sps.

Rnd 14: Join Dk Orange with dc in any ch-1 sp; 6 dc in same sp, skip next 2 dc, slip st **around** next slip st, ★ 7 dc in next ch-1 sp, skip next 2 dc, slip st **around** next slip st; repeat from ★ around; join with slip st to first dc, finish off: 154 dc and 22 slip sts.

Rnd 15: Join Lime with sc **around** any slip st; sc in Back Loops Only of next 7 dc, (sc **around** next slip st, sc in Back Loops Only of next 7 dc) around; join with slip st to first sc, finish off: 176 sc.

Rnd 16: Working in Back Loops Only, join Aqua with slip st in same st as joining; ch 4 (**counts as first tr**), ★ † dc in next sc, hdc in next sc, sc in next sc, slip st in next sc, sc in next sc, hdc in next sc, dc in next sc †, tr in next sc; repeat from ★ around to last 7 sts, then repeat from † to † once; join with slip st to first tr, finish off.

Rnd 17: Working in Back Loops Only, join Dk Orange with dc in any center slip st; dc in next 2 sts, ★ † skip next dc, work FPdc around next tr, dc in top of same tr, work FPdc around same tr, skip next dc †, dc in next 5 sts; repeat from ★ around to last 5 sts, then repeat from † to † once, dc in last 2 sts; join with slip st to first dc changing to Yellow, cut Dk Orange.

Rnd 18: Working in Back Loops Only, ch 3, dc in next dc and in each st around; join with slip st to first dc changing to Cream, cut Yellow.

Rnd 19: Working in Back Loops Only, ch 3, dc in next dc, work FPtr around first FPdc on Rnd 17, ★ skip next dc from last dc made, dc in next 3 dc, work FPtr around next FPdc on Rnd 17; repeat from ★ around to last 2 dc, skip next dc from last dc made, dc in last dc; join with slip st to first dc changing to Lime, cut Cream.

Rnd 20: Working in Back Loops Only, ch 3, dc in next 5 sts, place marker in last dc made, dc in next st and and in each st around; join with slip st to first dc, finish off.

Rnd 21: Working in Back Loops Only, join Aqua with dc in marked st; dc in next 2 dc, work split FPdtr, ★ skip next dc from last dc made, dc in next 7 dc, work split FPdtr; repeat from ★ around to last 5 dc, skip next dc from last dc made, dc in last 4 dc; join with slip st to first dc changing to Yellow, cut Aqua.

Rnd 22: Ch 1, work BPsc around same st as joining and each st around; join with slip st to **both** loops of first st, do **not** finish off.

Rnd 23: Ch 1, sc in same st as joining and in next 3 BPsc, ★ † skip next 3 BPsc, 10 tr in next BPsc, skip next 3 BPsc †, sc in next 4 BPsc; repeat from ★ around to last 7 BPsc, then repeat from † to † once; join with slip st to first sc changing to Dk Orange, cut Yellow: 224 sts.

Rnd 24: Ch 1, work BPsc around same st as joining and each of next 8 sts, (sc, ch 2, sc) in sp **before** next tr, place marker in same sp as first sc for st placement (**after** first sc), ★ work BPsc around each of next 14 sts, (sc, ch 2, sc) in sp **before** next tr; repeat from ★ around to last 5 tr, work BPsc around each of last 5 tr; join with slip st to first BPsc changing to Lime, cut Dk Orange: 256 sts and 16 ch-2 sps.

Rnd 25: Ch 1, sc in same st as joining, ★ † (ch 2, skip next 2 sts, sc in next st) twice, ch 3, skip next 3 sts, sc in next ch-2 sp, ch 3, skip next 3 sts, sc in next st, ch 2 †, skip next 2 sts, sc in next st; repeat from ★ 14 times **more**, then repeat from † to † once, skip last 2 sts; join with slip st to first sc, finish off: 80 sps.

Rnd 26: Join Cream with sc in first ch-2 sp; sc in same sp, ★ † 4 sc in each of next 2 sps, sc in next sc, work Picot, 4 sc in each of next 2 sps †, 3 sc in next ch-2 sp; repeat from ★ around to last 4 sps, then repeat from † to † once, sc in same sp as first sc; join with slip st changing to Aqua, cut Cream: 320 sc and 16 Picots.

Rnd 27: Ch 3, (2 dc, work Picot, 3 dc) in same st as joining, ch 4, keeping ch **behind** previous rnds, slip st **between** sc in marked sp, remove marker, ch 4, keeping ch **behind** previous rnds, ★ (3 dc, work Picot, 3 dc) in center sc of next 3-sc group, ch 4, keeping ch **behind** previous rnds, slip st **between** next 2 sc in sp between tr on Rnd 23, ch 4, keeping ch **behind** previous rnds; repeat from ★ around; join with slip st to first dc, finish off: 96 dc and 16 Picots.

Rnd 28: Join Lime with sc in any Picot on Rnd 26; ch 6, sc in next Picot on Rnd 27, ch 6, ★ sc in next Picot on Rnd 26, ch 6, sc in next Picot on Rnd 27, ch 6; repeat from ★ around; join with slip st to first sc, do **not** finish off: 32 sc and 32 ch-6 sps.

Rnd 29: Ch 1, sc in same st as joining, 7 sc in next ch-6 sp, (sc in next sc, 7 sc in next ch-6 sp) around; join with slip st to first sc: 256 sc.

Rnd 30: Ch 1, working from **left** to **right**, work reverse sc in each sc around *(Figs. 10a-d, page 63)*; join with slip st to first st, finish off.

TOWEL

●●○○ EASY

Finished Size:
17" x 16" (43 cm x 40.5 cm)

SHOPPING LIST

Yarn (Medium Weight)
[3.5 ounces, 186 yards
(100 grams, 170 meters) per skein]:
- ☐ White - 2 skeins
- ☐ Gray - 1 skein
- ☐ Yellow - 1 skein
- ☐ Green - 1 skein

Crochet Hook
- ☐ Size G (4 mm)
  or size needed for gauge

Additional Supplies
- ☐ Yarn needle

GAUGE INFORMATION
In Body pattern,
  17 sts and 10 rows = 4¼" (10.75 cm)
Gauge Swatch: 5½" (14 cm) square
Work same as Center Motif: 88 sc.

STITCH GUIDE
BEGINNING CLUSTER (uses one sp and one st)
Ch 2, ★ YO, insert hook in same sp **and** st as joining, YO and pull up a loop, YO and draw through 2 loops on hook; repeat from ★ once **more**, YO and draw through all 3 loops on hook.
CLUSTER (uses one sp and one st)
★ YO, insert hook in sp **and** through st indicated, YO and pull up a loop, YO and draw through 2 loops on hook; repeat from ★ 2 times **more**, YO and draw through all 4 loops on hook.
PUFF STITCH *(abbreviated Puff St)* (uses one st or sp)
★ YO, insert hook in st or sp indicated, YO and pull up a loop; repeat from ★ 3 times **more** (9 loops on hook), YO and draw through all 9 loops on hook, ch 1 to close.

CENTER MOTIF
Rnd 1 (Right side)**:** With White, ch 2, 8 hdc in second ch from hook; join with slip st to first hdc changing to Green *(Fig. 4a, page 61)*, cut White.

Note: Loop a short piece of yarn around any stitch to mark Rnd 1 as **right** side.

Rnd 2: Ch 2 (**does not count as a st, now and throughout**), work Puff St in first hdc, ch 1, (work Puff St in next hdc, ch 1) around; join with slip st to top of first Puff St, finish off: 8 Puff Sts and 8 ch-1 sps.

Rnd 3: With **right** side facing, join Yellow with dc in any ch-1 sp *(see Joining With Dc, page 60)*; (2 dc, ch 1, 3 dc) in same sp, ch 3, sc in next ch-1 sp, place marker in sc just made for st placement, ch 3, ★ (3 dc, ch 1, 3 dc) in next ch-1 sp, ch 3, sc in next ch-1 sp, ch 3; repeat from ★ 2 times **more**; join with slip st to first dc, finish off: 24 dc, 4 sc, and 12 sps.

Rnd 4: With **right** side facing and working **around** marked sc *(Fig. 8, page 62)*, join White with slip st in ch-1 sp on Rnd 2, do **not** remove marker, ★ † ch 3, 5 hdc in next ch-1 sp on Rnd 3, ch 3 †, slip st **around** next sc; repeat from ★ 2 times **more**, then repeat from † to † once; join with slip st to first slip st, finish off: 20 hdc, 4 slip sts, and 8 ch-3 sps.

Rnd 5: With **right** side facing, join Green with sc **around** first slip st *(see Joining With Sc, page 60)*; ★ † slip st in next 3 chs, sc in next 2 hdc, (slip st, ch 3, slip st) in next hdc, sc in next 2 hdc, slip st in next 3 chs †, sc **around** next slip st; repeat from ★ 2 times **more**, then repeat from † to † once; join with slip st to first sc, finish off: 4 corner ch-3 sps.

Rnd 6: With **right** side facing and working **behind** previous rnds, join White with dc in marked sc on Rnd 3; remove marker, (2 dc, ch 2, 3 dc) in same st, ch 4, ★ (3 dc, ch 2, 3 dc) in next sc on Rnd 3, ch 4; repeat from ★ 2 times **more**; join with slip st to first dc, finish off: 24 dc and 8 sps.

Rnd 7: With **right** side facing, join Yellow with slip st in any ch-4 sp, ch 2, 5 hdc in same sp, ★ † work (Puff St, ch 3, Puff St, ch 5, Puff St, ch 3, Puff St) in next ch-1 sp †, 5 hdc in next ch-4 sp; repeat from ★ 2 times **more**, then repeat from † to † once; join with slip st to first hdc, finish off: 20 hdc, 16 Puff Sts, and 12 sps.

SIDE MOTIF (Make 2)

Rnds 1-10: Work same as Center Motif, using Gray on Rnds 2 and 5 and Green on Rnd 8: 88 sc.

With **wrong** sides together, working in **both** loops of **both** pieces, and using White, whipstitch Side Motifs to Center Motif *(Fig. 11a, page 63)*, beginning in center sc of first corner 3-sc group and ending in center sc of next corner 3-sc group, forming a horizontal strip.

BODY

Row 1: With **right** side of one long edge of Motif strip facing, join White with slip st in center sc of first corner 3-sc group; ch 3 (**counts as first dc, now and throughout**), work 66 dc evenly spaced across: 67 dc.

Row 2: Ch 1, turn; (sc, 2 dc) in first dc, ★ skip next 2 dc, (sc, 2 dc) in next dc; repeat from ★ across to last 3 dc, skip next 2 dc, dc in last dc.

Row 3: Ch 3 (**counts as first dc**), turn; dc in next dc and in each st across.

Rows 4-27: Repeat Rows 2 and 3, 12 times.

Trim: Ch 1, do **not** turn; sc evenly across ends of rows to next Side Motif, sc in each sc across to center sc of next corner 3-sc group on same Motif, 3 sc in center sc, sc in each sc across to center sc of corner 3-sc group of next Side Motif, 3 sc in center sc, sc in each sc across same Motif; sc evenly across ends of rows; 3 sc in first dc on Row 27, sc in each dc across to last dc, 3 sc in last dc; join with slip st to first sc, finish off.

Rnd 8: With **right** side facing, holding any corner ch-3 sp on Rnd 5 in **front** of center hdc of 5-hdc group on Rnd 7, and working through **both** layers, join Gray with slip st, work (Beginning Cluster, ch 3, Cluster, ch 5, Cluster, ch 3, Cluster) in same sp, ★ † skip next Puff St, slip st in next ch-3 sp, working **behind** next ch-5 sp and **between** next 2 Puff Sts, (dc, ch 2, dc) in same sp as Puff Sts, slip st in next ch-3 sp †, holding next corner ch-3 sp on Rnd 5 in **front** of center hdc of 5-hdc group on Rnd 7 and working through **both** layers, work (Cluster, ch 3, Cluster, ch 5, Cluster ch 3, Cluster) in next sp; repeat from ★ 2 times **more**, then repeat from † to † once; join with slip st to top of Beginning Cluster, finish off: 16 Clusters, 16 sps and 8 dc.

Rnd 9: With **right** side facing, join White with sc in any corner ch-5 sp; ch 3, sc in same sp, ch 3, sc in next ch-3 sp, ★ † ch 4, holding ch-5 on Rnd 7 in **front** of next ch-2 and working in **both** sps, sc in next sp, ch 4, sc in next ch-3 sp, ch 3 †, (sc, ch 3) twice in next corner ch-5 sp, sc in next ch-3 sp; repeat from ★ 2 times **more**, then repeat from † to † once; join with slip st to first sc, do **not** finish off: 20 sps.

Rnd 10: Ch 1, sc in same st as joining, (3 sc in next ch-3 sp, sc in next sc) twice, (4 sc in next ch-4 sp, sc in next sc) twice, ★ (3 sc in next ch-3 sp, sc in next sc) 3 times, (4 sc in next ch-4 sp, sc in next sc) twice; repeat from ★ around to last ch-3 sp, 3 sc in last ch-3 sp; join with slip st to first sc, finish off: 88 sc.

PLACEMENT & COASTER SET

●●○○ EASY

Finished Sizes:
Placemat - 11" x 16" (28 cm x 40.5 cm)
Coaster - 5" (12.75 cm) diameter

SHOPPING LIST

Yarn (Medium Weight)
[1.75 ounces, 80 yards
(50 grams, 73 meters) per skein]:
☐ Coral - 2 skeins
☐ Aqua - 1 skein
☐ Yellow - 1 skein
☐ Tan - 1 skein
☐ Cream - 1 skein

Crochet Hook
☐ Size G (4 mm)
or size needed for gauge

Additional Supplies
☐ Yarn needle

GAUGE INFORMATION
In First Side pattern,
16 sc and 18 rows = 4" (10 cm)
Gauge Swatch: 4" (10 cm) diameter
Work same as Motif through Rnd 5: 40 dc
and 8 slip sts.

STITCH GUIDE
TREBLE CROCHET (abbreviated tr)
YO twice, insert hook in st indicated, YO and pull up a loop (4 loops on hook),
(YO and draw through 2 loops on hook) 3 times.
FRONT POST TREBLE CROCHET (abbreviated FPtr)
YO twice, insert hook from **front** to **back** around st indicated (Fig. 5,
page 61), YO and pull up a loop (4 loops on hook), (YO and draw through 2
loops on hook) 3 times. Skip sc behind FPtr.
FRONT POST DOUBLE CROCHET (abbreviated FPdc)
YO, insert hook from **front** to **back** around post of st indicated (Fig. 5, page
61), YO and pull up a loop (3 loops on hook), (YO and draw through 2 loops
on hook) twice. Skip sc behind FPdc.
BACK POST SINGLE CROCHET (abbreviated BPsc)
Insert hook from **back** to **front** around post of st indicated (Fig. 5, page 61),
YO and pull up a loop, YO and draw through both loops on hook.

PLACEMAT
MOTIF (Make 3)
Rnd 1 (Right side)**:** With Cream, ch 2,
8 hdc in second ch from hook; join with
slip st to first hdc; finish off.

Note: Loop a short piece of yarn around
any stitch to mark Rnd 1 as **right** side.

Rnd 2: With **right** side facing, join Yellow
with slip st in any hdc; ch 8, slip st in
same st, (slip st, ch 8, slip st) in next hdc
and in each hdc around; do **not** join:
64 chs.

Rnd 3: Skip joining slip st, ★ slip st in top
loops of first 4 chs of next ch-8 (Fig. 2,
page 60), ch 2, slip st in top loops of next
4 chs, skip next 2 slip sts; repeat from
★ around; join with slip st to first ch,
finish off: 8 ch-2 sps.

Rnd 4: With **right** side facing, join Aqua
with sc in any ch-2 sp (see Joining With
Sc, page 60); ch 1, skip next 4 slip sts,
(tr, ch 1) twice in next slip st, ★ sc in
next ch-2 sp, ch 1, skip next 4 slip sts, (tr,
ch 1) twice in next slip st; repeat from
★ around; join with slip st to first sc,
finish off: 16 tr, 8 sc, and 24 ch-1 sps.

Rnd 5: With **right** side facing, join Coral with slip st in any sc; skip next ch-1 sp, 5 dc in next ch-1 sp, skip next tr, ★ slip st in next sc, skip next ch-1 sp, 5 dc in next ch-1 sp, skip next tr; repeat from ★ around; join with slip st to joining slip st, finish off: 40 dc and 8 slip sts.

Rnd 6: With **right** side facing, join Tan with dc in same st as joining *(see Joining With Dc, page 60)*; (dc, ch 2, 2 dc) in same st, slip st in Back Loop Only of center dc on next 5-dc group *(Fig. 3, page 60)*, ★ (2 dc, ch 2, 2 dc) in **both** loops of next slip st, slip st in Back Loop Only of center dc on next 5-dc group; repeat from ★ around; join with slip st to **both** loops of first dc, finish off: 32 dc, 8 slip sts, and 8 corner ch-2 sps.

Rnd 7: With **right** side facing, join Yellow with dc in any corner ch-2 sp; (2 dc, ch 2, 3 dc) in same sp ★ †, ch 3, skip next ch-2 sp, working **behind** previous rnds, slip st in sc on Rnd 4 **below** skipped ch-2 sp, ch 3 †, (3 dc, ch 2, 3 dc) in next ch-2 sp; repeat from ★ 2 times **more**, then repeat from † to † once; join with slip st to first dc, finish off: 24 dc, 8 ch-3 sps, and 4 corner ch-2 sps.

Rnd 8: With **right** side facing, join Cream with dc in any corner ch-2 sp; (dc, ch 2, 2 dc) in same sp, ★ † dc in next 3 dc, 3 dc in next ch-3 sp, slip st in next skipped ch-2 sp on Rnd 6, 3 dc in next ch-3 sp on Rnd 7, dc in next 3 dc †, (2 dc, ch 2, 2 dc) in next corner ch-2 sp; repeat from ★ 2 times **more**, then repeat from † to † once; join with slip st to first dc, finish off: 64 dc, 4 slip sts, and 4 corner ch-2 sps.

Rnd 9: With **right** side facing, join Coral with BPsc around first dc *(see Joining With BPsc, page 60)*; work BPsc around next dc, ch 2, skip next corner ch-2 sp,

★ work BPsc around each st across to next corner ch-2 sp, ch 2, skip corner ch-2 sp; repeat from ★ 2 times **more**, work BPsc around each st across; join with slip st to first BPsc, finish off: 68 sc and 4 ch-2 sps.

With **wrong** sides together, using Coral, and working through inside loops, whipstitch Motifs together *(Fig. 11b, page 63)*, beginning in second ch of first corner ch-2 sp and ending in first ch of next corner ch-2 sp, forming a horizontal strip of 3 Motifs.

FIRST SIDE

Row 1: With **right** side of one long edge of Center facing, join Coral with sc in second ch of first corner ch-2 sp; work 61 sc evenly spaced across: 62 sc.

Row 2: Ch 1, turn; sc in each sc across.

Row 3: Ch 1, turn; sc in first 3 sc, skip first 3 sc on Row 1, work FPdc around each of next 2 sc, ★ sc in next 4 sc, skip 4 sc from last FPdc made, work FPdc around each of next 2 sc; repeat from ★ across to last 3 sc, sc in last 3 sc: 42 sc and 20 FPdc.

Row 4: Ch 1, turn; sc in each st across.

Row 5: Ch 1, turn; sc in first sc, work FPtr around first FPdc **below**, sc in next 4 sc, ★ work FPtr around next 2 FPdc **below**, sc in next 4 sc; repeat from ★ across to last sc, work FPtr around last FPdc **below**, sc in last sc.

Row 6: Ch 1, turn; sc in each st across.

Row 7: Ch 1, turn; sc in first sc, work FPdc around first FPtr **below**, sc in next 4 sc, ★ work FPdc around each of next 2 FPtr **below**, sc in next 4 sc; repeat from ★ across to last sc, work FPdc around last FPtr **below**, sc in last sc.

Row 8: Ch 1, turn; sc in each st across.

Row 9: Ch 1, turn; sc in first sc, work FPdc around first FPdc **below** next sc, sc in next 4 sc, ★ work FPdc around each FPdc **below** next 2 sc, sc in next 4 sc; repeat from ★ across to last 2 sc, work FPdc around last FPdc **below** next sc, sc in last sc.

Row 10: Ch 1, turn; sc in each st across.

Row 11: Ch 1, turn; sc in first 3 sc, ★ work FPtr around each FPdc **below**, sc in next 4 sc; repeat from ★ across to last 3 sc, sc in last 3 sc.

Row 12: Ch 1, turn; sc in each st across.

Row 13: Ch 1, turn; sc in first 3 sc, work FPdc around each FPtr **below** next 2 sc, ★ sc in next 4 sc, work FPdc around each FPtr **below** next 2 sc; repeat from ★ across to last 3 sc, sc in last 3 sc.

Row 14: Ch 1, turn; sc in each st across; finish off.

SECOND SIDE

Row 1: With **right** side of remaining long edge of Center facing, join Coral with sc in second ch of first corner ch-2 sp; work 61 sc evenly spaced across: 62 sc.

Rows 2-14: Work same as First Side; at end of Row 14, do **not** finish off.

TRIM

Ch 1, turn; 3 sc in first sc, sc in each sc across to last sc, 3 sc in last sc; sc evenly across ends of rows on Second Side; † working across next Motif, sc in next corner ch and in each BPsc across to next corner ch, sc in corner ch †; sc evenly

across ends of rows on First Side; 3 sc in first sc, sc in each sc across to last sc, 3 sc in last sc, sc evenly across ends of rows on First Side, repeat from † to † once; sc evenly across ends of rows on Second Side; join with slip st to first sc, finish off.

COASTER

Rnds 1-5: Work same as Motif Center: 40 dc and 8 slip sts.

Rnd 6: With **right** side facing, join Cream with slip st in same st as joining; ch 3, 6 dc in same st, slip st in Back Loop Only of center dc of next 5-dc group, ★ 7 dc in **both** loops of next slip st, slip st in Back Loop Only of center dc of next 5-dc group; repeat from ★ around; join with slip st to **both** loops of first dc, finish off.

GENERAL INSTRUCTIONS

ABBREVIATIONS

BPdc	Back Post double crochet(s)
BPsc	Back Post single crochet(s)
ch(s)	chain(s)
cm	centimeters
dc	double crochet(s)
dc2tog	double crochet 2 together
dc3tog	double crochet 3 together
dtr	double treble crochet(s)
FPdc	Front Post double crochet(s)
FPdtr	Front Post double treble crochet(s)
FPsc	Front Post single crochet(s)
FPtr	Front Post treble crochet(s)
hdc	half double crochet(s)
mm	millimeters
Rnd(s)	Round(s)
sc	single crochet(s)
sp(s)	space(s)
st(s)	stitch(es)
tr	treble crochet(s)
YO	yarn over

SYMBOLS & TERMS

★ — work instructions following ★ as many **more** times as indicated in addition to the first time.

† to † — work all instructions from first † to second † **as many** times as specified.

( ) or **[ ]** — work enclosed instructions **as many** times as specified by the number immediately following **or** work all enclosed instructions in the stitch or space indicated **or** contains explanatory remarks.

colon (:) — the number(s) given after a colon at the end of a row or round denote(s) the number of stitches and spaces you should have on that row or round.

CROCHET TERMINOLOGY		
UNITED STATES		INTERNATIONAL
slip stitch (slip st)	=	single crochet (sc)
single crochet (sc)	=	double crochet (dc)
half double crochet (hdc)	=	half treble crochet (htr)
double crochet (dc)	=	treble crochet (tr)
treble crochet (tr)	=	double treble crochet (dtr)
double treble crochet (dtr)	=	triple treble crochet (ttr)
triple treble crochet (tr tr)	=	quadruple treble crochet (qtr)
skip	=	miss

●○○○ BASIC	Projects using basic stitches. May include basic increases and decreases.
●●○○ EASY	Projects may include simple stitch patterns, color work, and/or shaping.
●●●○ INTERMEDIATE	Projects may include involved stitch patterns, color work, and/or shaping.
●●●● COMPLEX	Projects may include complex stitch patterns, color work, and/or shaping using a variety of techniques and stitches simultaneously.

CROCHET HOOKS																
U.S.	B-1	C-2	D-3	E-4	F-5	G-6	7	H-8	I-9	J-10	K-10½	L-11	M/N-13	N/P-15	P/Q	Q	S
Metric - mm	2.25	2.75	3.25	3.5	3.75	4	4.5	5	5.5	6	6.5	8	9	10	15	16	19

Yarn Weight Symbol & Names	LACE 0	SUPER FINE 1	FINE 2	LIGHT 3	MEDIUM 4	BULKY 5	SUPER BULKY 6	JUMBO 7
Type of Yarns in Category	Fingering, size 10 crochet thread	Sock, Fingering, Baby	Sport, Baby	DK, Light Worsted	Worsted, Afghan, Aran	Chunky, Craft, Rug	Super Bulky, Roving	Jumbo, Roving
Crochet Gauge* Ranges in Single Crochet to 4" (10 cm)	32-42 sts**	21-32 sts	16-20 sts	12-17 sts	11-14 sts	8-11 sts	6-9 sts	5 sts and fewer
Advised Hook Size Range	Steel*** 6 to 8, Regular hook B-1	B-1 to E-4	E-4 to 7	7 to I-9	I-9 to K-10½	K-10½ to M/N-13	M/N-13 to Q	Q and larger

*GUIDELINES ONLY: The chart above reflects the most commonly used gauges and hook sizes for specific yarn categories.

** Lace weight yarns are usually crocheted with larger hooks to create lacy openwork patterns. Accordingly, a gauge range is difficult to determine. Always follow the gauge stated in your pattern.

*** Steel crochet hooks are sized differently from regular hooks–the higher the number, the smaller the hook, which is the reverse of regular hook sizing.

GAUGE

Exact gauge is **essential** for proper size. Before beginning your project, make the sample swatch given in the individual instructions in the yarn and hook specified. After completing the swatch, measure it, counting your stitches and rows or rounds carefully. If your swatch is larger or smaller than specified, **make another, changing hook size to get the correct gauge**. Keep trying until you find the size hook that will give you the specified gauge.

MARKERS

Markers are used to help distinguish the beginning of each round being worked. Place a 2" (5 cm) scrap piece of yarn before the first stitch of each round, moving marker after each round is complete.

JOINING WITH SC

When instructed to join with sc, begin with a slip knot on hook. Insert hook in stitch or space indicated, YO and pull up a loop, YO and draw through both loops on hook.

JOINING WITH DC

When instructed to join with hdc, begin with a slip knot on hook. YO, holding loop on hook, insert hook in stitch or space indicated, YO and pull up a loop (3 loops on hook), (YO and draw through 2 loops on hook) twice.

JOINING WITH BPSC

When instructed to join with BPsc, begin with a slip knot on hook. Insert hook from **back** to **front** around post of stitch indicated, YO and pull up a loop, YO and draw through both loops on hook.

BACK RIDGE

Work only in loops indicated by arrows *(Fig. 1)*.

TOP LOOPS

Work only in loops indicated by arrow *(Fig. 2)*.

BACK LOOP ONLY

Work only in loop(s) indicated by arrow *(Fig. 3)*.

Fig. 1

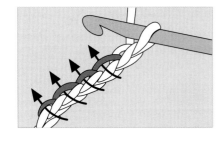

Fig. 2

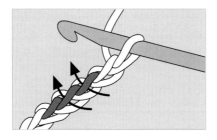

Fig. 3

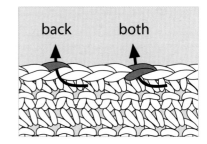

FREE LOOPS

After working in Back Loops Only on a row or round, there will be a ridge of unused loops. These are called the free loops. Later, when instructed to work in the free loops of the same row or round, work in these loops *(Fig. 4a)*.

When instructed to work in free loops of a chain, work in loop indicated by arrow *(Fig. 4b)*.

Fig. 4a

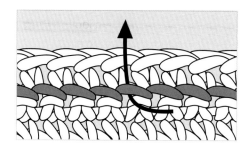

Fig. 4b

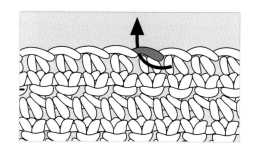

POST STITCH

Work around post of stitch indicated, inserting hook in direction of arrow *(Fig. 5)*.

Fig. 5

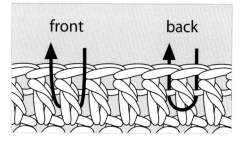

CHANGING COLORS

To change colors while joining with a slip st, drop yarn, insert hook in first st, hook new yarn and draw through st and loop on hook *(Fig. 6a)*.

Fig. 6a

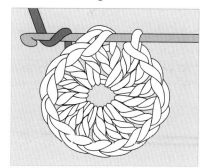

To change colors at the end of row, work last st to within one step of completion, drop yarn, with new yarn, YO and draw through remaining 2 loops on hook *(Fig. 6b)*. Do **not** cut old yarn unless instructed.

Fig. 6b

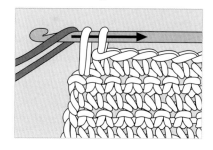

WORKING IN SPACE BEFORE A STITCH

When instructed to work in space **before** a stitch or in spaces **between** stitches, insert hook in space indicated by arrow (*Fig. 7*).

WORKING IN FRONT OF, AROUND, OR BEHIND A STITCH

Work in stitch or space indicated, inserting hook in direction of arrow (*Fig. 8*).

WORKING IN HORIZONTAL BAR

When instructed to work in horizontal bar of hdc, work in loop indicated by arrow (*Fig. 9*).

Fig. 7

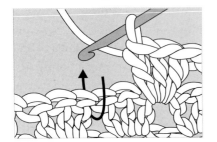

Fig. 8

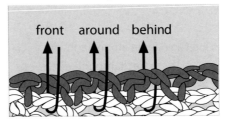

front   around   behind

Fig. 9

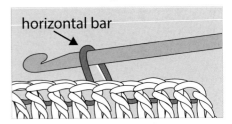

horizontal bar

REVERSE SINGLE CROCHET

(abbreviated reverse sc)

Working from **left** to **right**, ★ insert hook in st to right of hook *(Fig. 10a)*, YO and draw through, under and to left of loop on hook (2 loops on hook) *(Fig. 10b)*, YO and draw through both loops on hook *(Fig. 10c)* **(reverse sc made, *Fig. 10d*)**; repeat from ★ around.

Fig. 10a

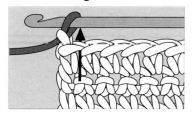

Fig. 10b

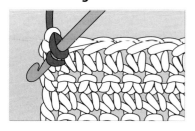

Fig. 10c

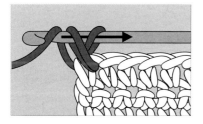

Fig. 10d

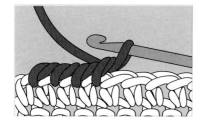

WHIPSTITCH

Place two Motifs with **wrong** sides together. Beginning in corner ch or st specified, sew through both pieces once to secure the beginning of the seam, leaving an ample yarn end to weave in later. Insert the needle from **front** to **back** through **both** loops on **both** pieces **or** through **inside** loops only of each stitch on **both** pieces) *(Fig. 11a or b)*. Bring the needle around and insert it from **front** to **back** through next loops of both pieces. Continue in this manner across, keeping the sewing yarn fairly loose.

Fig. 11a

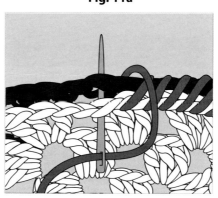

Fig. 11b

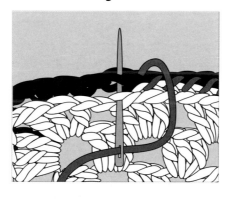

TASSEL

Cut a piece of cardboard 3" (7.5 cm) wide and as long as you want your finished tassel to be. Wind a double strand of yarn around the cardboard as many times as specified. Cut a 12" (30.5 cm) length of yarn and insert it under all of the strands at the top of the cardboard; pull up **tightly** and tie securely. Cut the yarn at the opposite end of the cardboard and then remove it *(Fig. 12a)*. Cut a 6" (15 cm) length of yarn and wrap it **tightly** around the tassel twice, 1" (2.5 cm) below the top *(Fig. 12b)*; tie securely. Trim the ends.

Fig. 12a

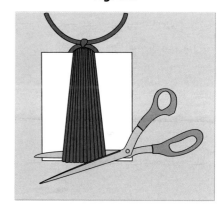

Fig. 12b

YARN INFORMATION

Each item in this book was made using Medium Weight Yarn. Any brand of Medium Weight Yarn may be used. It is best to refer to the yardage/meters when determining how many balls or skeins to purchase. Remember, to arrive at the finished size, it is the GAUGE/TENSION that is important, not the brand of yarn.

For your convenience, listed below are the specific yarns used to create our photography models. Because yarn manufacturers make frequent changes to their product lines, you may sometimes find it necessary to use a substitute yarn or to search for the discontinued product at alternate suppliers (locally or online).

BASKET
Red Heart® Scrubby Smoothie™
Cream - #9313 Loofah
Coral - #9327 Coral
Blue - #9287 Caribbean

BLANKET
Bernat® Handicrafter® Cotton
White - #01001 White
Aqua - #01215 Robins Egg
Coral - #01746 Coral Rose
Yellow - #01030 Pale Yellow

CROSSBODY BAG
Bernat® Handicrafter® Cotton
Violet - #01097 Soft Violet
Coral - #01746 Coral Rose
Yellow - #01030 Pale Yellow
Cream - #01002 Off White

MANDALA
Lion Brand® 24/7 Cotton®
Aqua - #102 Aqua
White - #100 White
Pink - #101 Pink
Rose - #144 Magenta
Orange - #133 Tangerine

PILLOW
Lion Brand® 24/7 Cotton®
Lilac - #143 Lilac
Green - #156 Mint
Dk Green - #178 Jade
Cream - #098 Ecru
Gold - #158 Goldenrod

POUF
Bernat® Handicrafter® Cotton
Cream - #01002 Soft White
Violet - #01097 Soft Violet
Dk Violet - #01317 Hot Purple
Tan - #01085 Jute

DOILY RUG
Lily® Sugar'n Cream®
Yellow - #00010 Yellow
Aqua - #01132 Beach Glass
Dk Orange - #01699 Tangerine
Lime - #01712 Hot Green
Cream - #01004 Soft Ecru

TOWEL
Lion Brand® 24/7 Cotton®
White - #100 White
Gray - #149 Silver
Green - #172 Grass
Yellow - #157 Lemon

PLACEMAT & COASTER SET
Bernat® Handicrafter® Cotton
Coral - #01746 Coral Rose
Aqua - #01215 Robins Egg
Yellow - #01030 Pale Yellow
Tan - #01085 Jute
Cream - #01002 Off White

We have made every effort to ensure that these instructions are accurate and complete. We cannot, however, be responsible for human error, typographical mistakes, or variations in individual work.

Production Team: Instructional/Technical Editor - Sarah J. Green; Senior Graphic Artist - Lora Puls; Photo Stylist - Lori Wenger; and Photographer - Jason Masters.

Library of Congress Control Number: 2019933138

Made in U.S.A.